AI-Native Software Delivery
Proven Practices to Produce
High-Quality Software Faster

Nick Durkin, Eric Minick, and Chinmay Gaikwad

O'REILLY®

AI-Native Software Delivery
by Nick Durkin, Eric Minick, and Chinmay Gaikwad

Copyright © 2025 O'Reilly Media, Inc. All rights reserved.

Published by O'Reilly Media, Inc., 141 Stony Circle, Suite 195, Santa Rosa, CA 95401.

O'Reilly books may be purchased for educational, business, or sales promotional use. Online editions are also available for most titles (*http://oreilly.com*). For more information, contact our corporate/institutional sales department: 800-998-9938 or *corporate@oreilly.com*.

Acquisitions Editor: Louise Corrigan	**Indexer:** Potomac Indexing, LLC
Development Editor: Jeff Bleiel	**Cover Designer:** Karen Montgomery
Production Editor: Elizabeth Faerm	**Cover Illustrator:** José Marzan Jr.
Copyeditor: J.M. Olejarz	**Interior Designer:** David Futato
Proofreader: Krsta Technology Solutions	**Interior Illustrator:** Kate Dullea

August 2025:   First Edition

Revision History for the First Edition
2025-07-25:   First Release

See *http://oreilly.com/catalog/errata.csp?isbn=9781098171995* for release details.

978-1-098-17199-5

[LSI]

Table of Contents

Preface

The software industry stands at a pivotal moment. Systems grow more complex by the day, user demands escalate exponentially, and the cost of failure, whether financial, reputational, or operational, has never been higher. Yet despite decades of progress, many teams remain shackled to outdated practices: manual deployments, reactive firefighting, and toolchains that crumble under their own complexity. This book exists to bridge the gap between where we are and where we need to be. It's a map for navigating the shift from brittle, high-stakes delivery to AI-driven autonomy—a future where software deploys itself, systems self-heal, and innovation outpaces risk.

Who Should Read This Book

This book is written for:

- Engineers and DevOps practitioners, seeking to replace toil with intelligent automation
- Technical leaders, tasked with aligning DevOps maturity with business outcomes like velocity, resilience, and cost control
- Product managers and innovators, who want to understand how AI-native delivery accelerates time-to-value
- Anyone invested in the future of software, from CTOs to students, ready to rethink what's possible in deployment, testing, and observability

Why We Wrote This Book

As software engineers by training, we've spent years studying the evolution of software development and delivery. But OpenAI's launch of ChatGPT in late 2022 marked a pivotal moment for us. Like many in the field, we saw generative AI not just as a coding assistant but as a catalyst for reimagining entire delivery pipelines.

Over the next three years, we hypothesized, tested, and validated how AI, from code generation to agentic workflows, would reshape deployment, testing, and governance.

We wrote this book because the stakes of software delivery have changed. The rise of microservices, cloud-native architectures, and AI-generated code has rendered traditional DevOps 1.0 practices insufficient. Teams now juggle 10+ tools in a single pipeline, battle "dependency hell," and face threats like SolarWinds-style supply chain attacks, all while racing to meet user expectations forged by consumer tech giants.

Existing resources focus on historical DevOps concepts or speculate about AI in abstract terms. This book connects the dots. Grounded in 25 years of lessons, from Agile's early wins to the Kubernetes orchestration revolution, we pair technical rigor with forward-looking insights. Modern tools exemplify this shift. We show how AI isn't just automating tasks but reshaping collaboration, governance, and innovation.

Of course, the pace of change is relentless. Agentic AI, self-operating systems, and new frameworks emerge monthly. While we've strived to future-proof this book, we acknowledge that some details will evolve. What won't change are the core principles: automating toil, prioritizing resilience, and aligning delivery with business value.

Navigating This Book

This book isn't about chasing trends. It's about building systems that thrive amid complexity. Each chapter blends theory with real-world examples, from *The Phoenix Project*'s DevOps parable to AI-driven deployment. Whether you read cover-to-cover or dive into specific sections, you'll finish equipped to transform your delivery process and your team's impact.

Chapter 1, "The Road to AI-Native DevOps", traces software delivery's evolution from chaotic manual deployments to DevOps 1.0 practices (with their cultural shifts and automation tools) while highlighting current challenges from microservices complexity and toolchain sprawl that DevOps 2.0 aims to solve through AI-native capabilities and integrated platforms.

Chapter 2, "Source Control Management", traces the evolution of source control management (SCM) from early systems to Git's current dominance (with nearly 95% of developers using it as of 2022), explaining how modern SCM solves code conflicts and version tracking while providing practical guidance on branching strategies, GitOps, AI integration, and implementation considerations for your organization.

Chapter 3, "The Build and Pre-Deployment Testing Steps of Continuous Integration", explores the evolution of continuous integration (CI) from its historical roots to modern AI-enhanced practices, detailing how to build automation, intelligent caching, and strategic testing approaches work together to accelerate software delivery while maintaining quality and security throughout the pre-deployment pipeline.

Chapter 4, "Deploying to Test Environments", guides you through the critical phase between CI and production deployment, exploring how to establish consistent deployment processes across environments, leverage Infrastructure as Code (IaC) for reliability, implement GitOps workflows, optimize testing strategies (including emerging AI-powered approaches), and automate promotion decisions—all to create a seamless bridge between development and real-world usage while maintaining both velocity and stability.

Chapter 5, "Securing Applications and the Software Supply Chain", looks at the evolving landscape of software supply chain security, detailing how organizations can protect their applications through shift-left practices, Supply Chain Levels for Software Artifacts (SLSA) frameworks, software bills of materials (SBOMs), and AI-enhanced security tools while fostering a collaborative DevSecOps culture that integrates security throughout the entire software development lifecycle (SDLC).

Chapter 6, "Chaos Engineering and Service Reliability", explores chaos engineering as a methodical approach to building resilient systems, showing how controlled failure experiments—from simple latency tests to complex infrastructure disruptions—can be integrated with service-level objectives (SLOs), error budgets, and continuous integration and continuous delivery (CI/CD) pipelines to create a culture of continuous resilience that transforms unpredictable outages into anticipated, manageable events.

Chapter 7, "Deploying to Production", digs into the critical challenges of production deployments through the lens of a real-life case study, offering a comprehensive framework for modern deployment governance, progressive delivery strategies, and AI-enhanced verification techniques that together transform high-risk deployments into controlled, observable, and reversible processes that protect both your application and your business.

Chapter 8, "Feature Management and Experimentation", covers how feature management and experimentation serve as cornerstones of modern software delivery, showing how feature flags enable trunk-based development, team decoupling, and progressive delivery while AI-enhanced experimentation transforms product decisions from subjective debates into data-driven insights that maximize business value.

Chapter 9, "AI and Automation for Cloud Cost Management", looks at the complex world of cloud cost management, tracing its evolution into FinOps practices, examining multicloud challenges, and demonstrating how AI-powered solutions can optimize resource allocation, enforce governance policies, and align cost efficiency with business objectives and environmental sustainability goals.

Chapter 10, "A Platform Engineering Approach to Modern DevOps", explores how platform engineering addresses the developer cognitive load crisis by creating integrated, self-service platforms that provide paved roads and standardized templates, enabling organizations to balance developer productivity with governance requirements while treating the platform as a product with developers as its customers—all illustrated through a practical case study of a financial services organization that transformed its delivery capabilities with just 6 platform engineers serving 1,400 developers.

Conventions Used in This Book

The following typographical conventions are used in this book:

Italic
> Indicates new terms, URLs, email addresses, filenames, and file extensions.

> This element signifies a general note.

O'Reilly Online Learning

For more than 40 years, *O'Reilly Media* has provided technology and business training, knowledge, and insight to help companies succeed.

Our unique network of experts and innovators share their knowledge and expertise through books, articles, and our online learning platform. O'Reilly's online learning platform gives you on-demand access to live training courses, in-depth learning paths, interactive coding environments, and a vast collection of text and video from O'Reilly and 200+ other publishers. For more information, visit *https://oreilly.com*.

How to Contact Us

Please address comments and questions concerning this book to the publisher:

> O'Reilly Media, Inc.
> 141 Stony Circle, Suite 195
> Santa Rosa, CA 95401
> 800-889-8969 (in the United States or Canada)
> 707-827-7019 (international or local)
> 707-829-0104 (fax)
> *support@oreilly.com*
> *https://oreilly.com/about/contact.html*

We have a web page for this book, where we list errata, examples, and any additional information. You can access this page at *https://oreil.ly/ai-native-software-delivery*.

For news and information about our books and courses, visit *https://oreilly.com*.

Find us on LinkedIn: *https://linkedin.com/company/oreilly-media*.

Watch us on YouTube: *https://youtube.com/oreillymedia*.

Acknowledgments

We owe a profound debt of gratitude to many individuals whose expertise, encouragement, and unwavering support transformed this book from a bold idea into reality.

Special thanks to our excellent colleagues for providing the subject matter expertise: Matthew Schillerstrom, David Karow, Mridhula Venkat, Dan Gordan, Sean Roth, Harold Bell, and Patrick Wolf.

We also thank the book's technical reviewers—Charles Humble, Julian Setiawan, Sagar Gandhi, and Laura Uzcategui—for their valuable feedback on the technical aspects of the book.

Thanks also to the O'Reilly team who worked with us throughout this rewarding process: acquisitions editor Louise Corrigan, development editor Jeff Bleiel, production editor Elizabeth Faerm, and managing editor Lisa LaRew.

Thanks also to Kristy Saunders.

CHAPTER 1

The Road to AI-Native DevOps

Most software development teams can tell war stories about deployments gone wrong. These are the stories that put us on paths to modernize our delivery practices.

Here's one: After weeks or months of feature work, extensive refactoring, and a long testing and stabilization phase, a team is ready to deploy. Developers, operations team members, a coterie of managers, and maybe a number of executives gather in a "war room." Up to this point, there has been minimal collaboration between development and operations. However, now these two groups are working together as a single team. They start ticking through a long checklist or playbook of manual steps.

However, even exhaustive checklists do not guarantee a problem-free deployment. Given the number of changes in the release, the deployment is likely complex and risky. As we will see in the following chapters, dependency management is challenging and "dependency hell" can be very real. So, the team might find that a key dependency was missing from the production environment. The team might discover that an incompatible library version was installed, or that a critical setting was misconfigured, or that a migration step fails or is forgotten, or that changes have caused requests to a partner service to fail.

Any number of missteps could take an already complex deployment off track. Tensions would rise, firefighting would ensue, and the hours would stretch on. The team would hope to wrap up deployment and any subsequent manual smoke testing within the deployment window. If the deployment failed irreparably and could not be salvaged, the team would hope that a rollback to the previous version would not result in unexpected difficulties, extending downtime and complexity. When the deployment is finally complete, the exhausted team retreats. Often the team would be expected to be vigilant as traffic resumed for the span of a "critical care period." A stabilization period of a few days or weeks might follow in which the development team might pause all feature work to focus on hotfixes or patches.

As this story illustrates, heavy-lift, high-stakes deployments were draining for both the development and operations teams. These big-production deployments, followed by cycles of stabilization work, distracted teams from continuing to build features that added business value.

In contrast, modern software delivery streamlines and accelerates the entire process of getting software from the developer's computer to the end user. Deployments are frequent, low drama, low risk, and highly automated. But we're entering a new era— one that goes beyond automation. The next frontier is AI-native software delivery.

AI-native delivery weaves AI into every layer of the software delivery lifecycle, enabling intelligent agents to make decisions, optimize workflows, and adapt in real time. These agents—ranging from Code and DevOps to Security and Test—collaborate autonomously, enforce compliance, self-heal infrastructure, and continuously optimize software delivery pipelines using reinforcement learning. This shift marks a move from reactive to proactive governance, from siloed tools to unified ecosystems, and from static automation to dynamic autonomy.

As AI generates code, orchestrates pipelines, and reduces manual toil, development velocity accelerates. Systems become more resilient and secure, with AI preemptively identifying issues and autonomously resolving them. At the same time, cloud costs shrink through intelligent optimization, and collaboration scales as AI-powered agents handle cross-team coordination and decision-making at machine speed.

In this chapter, we will describe how software delivery has evolved over the past 25 years. We will define DevOps and describe how DevOps practices enable modern software delivery. We will look at numerous challenges to the current state of DevOps. Lastly, this chapter will provide an overview of how modern software delivery, DevOps practices, and an AI-native approach can evolve to meet these challenges.

Development + Operations = DevOps

The term "DevOps'" is often attributed to Patrick Debois, who in 2009 combined the words "development" and "operations'" to name a conference he organized to explore breaking down the traditional walls between development and operations teams to deliver software faster. Two main factors created these walls:

Poor communication and collaboration
> Developers commonly focused on writing code and features, then essentially threw the finished product over a metaphorical wall to the Ops team. Ops then bore the responsibility of deploying, maintaining, and troubleshooting the code in production.

Conflicting priorities

Development teams prioritized rapid development and the quick release of new features, while Ops teams focused on system stability, security, and preventing downtime. Despite their different priorities, these teams are inherently interconnected and interdependent. No matter how impressive your code or infrastructure is, it has no real value until it's deployed and running in production to serve your business objectives.

This goal mismatch, sometimes referred to as "the core chronic conflict," could lead to friction and finger-pointing when issues arise.

In response, DevOps principles encourage communication at every stage. They encourage Ops involvement early in development and an ongoing partnership with Devs in supporting code long after it has been deployed.

A Short History of DevOps

Increasingly sophisticated software teams, new software methodologies, and new tools helped pave the way for DevOps. In this section we'll look at these factors.

Agile in the Aughts

In the early 2000s, organizations became very interested in and receptive to new ideas about how to make software delivery more efficient. New "Agile" methodologies that built on lean manufacturing ideas became popular. These methodologies argued against "waterfall" software delivery patterns that emphasized extensive up-front planning and a strictly linear sequence of distinct phases. In contrast, Agile promoted short development cycles and frequent releases that were highly responsive to change. Many parallel efforts formalized new Agile practices. A 1995 paper formalized Scrum practices. Kent Beck described a set of Agile practices for software development in his 1999 book *Extreme Programming Explained* (Addison-Wesley). In 2001, Beck and other influential advocates of Agile processes spoke to similar themes in the Agile Manifesto, which promoted adaptability and responsiveness over rigid adherence to plans.[1] DevOps borrows the name "continuous delivery" from the manifesto's first principle: "Our highest priority is to satisfy the customer through early and continuous delivery of valuable software."

Jeffrey Fredrick has observed that the progression of Ken Schwaber's Scrum books from 2001 to 2007 serves as a kind of barometer for Agile's increasing maturity and organizational reach. During this time, Scrum was rapidly emerging as the dominant Agile practice, thanks to its clear structure, prescriptive roles, and adaptability across

---

1 Kent Beck et al., "Manifesto for Agile Software Development" (*https://agilemanifesto.org*), 2001, Agile Alliance. Retrieved 14 June 2010.

teams. In 2001, *Agile Software Development with Scrum* (Pearson) introduced the framework to developers and small teams just beginning to explore Agile methods. By 2004, *Agile Project Management with Scrum* (Addison-Wesley) addressed practical implementation challenges, signaling growing adoption across broader swaths of IT. By 2007, *The Enterprise and Scrum* (Microsoft Press) acknowledged the growing demand for scaling Agile practices beyond individual teams to entire organizations. These books reflected—and helped shape—the journey of Agile from fringe idea to enterprise imperative.

Continuous Integration and Continuous Delivery

Over the next decade, technology organizations were increasingly influenced by agile thinking. One result was the adoption of continuous integration and continuous delivery (CI/CD) practices.

The "Manifesto for Agile Software Development" gave rise to the practice of continuous integration, which enables a key agile tenet, the frequent delivery of working software. Developers merge their code changes into a shared repository. With continuous integration, each merge triggers an automated build and testing process. This automated system quickly catches errors and conflicts, allowing teams to fix them early in the development cycle. Continuous integration encourages smaller, more frequent updates, leading to faster delivery, reduced integration issues, and a healthier codebase.

Continuous delivery is a natural extension of continuous integration. CD automates the process of taking code that has passed the integration build and testing and preparing it for release to production environments. This includes steps like packaging, configuring, and deploying the software to staging areas. CD enables teams to push new features, bug fixes, and updates rapidly and reliably, ensuring that deployable software is always available.

Delivering a "potentially shippable product" at the conclusion of each development cycle is another key Agile practice. Potentially shippable simply means reliable, tested, packaged software that could be deployed to production. (In practice, many organizations that embraced CD delivered only internally and continued to deploy to production infrequently. Continuous delivery did not equal continuous deployment.)

Milestones in Early DevOps

Whereas Agile methodologies tend to focus on the planning and execution parts of the software delivery lifecycle, early DevOps focused on delivery and operations. In the years that followed the emergence of DevOps, the movement gained significant momentum. A key milestone occurred in 2009, when the inaugural DevOpsDays conference was held. This event brought together professionals to share their experiences and insights on DevOps practices.

Another significant development was the 2010 publication of the book *The Phoenix Project* (IT Revolution Press) by Gene Kim, Kevin Behr, and George Spafford. This narrative illustrated the challenges faced by a fictional IT organization and how the adoption of DevOps principles and practices led to a dramatic turnaround in its performance. It made the case for DevOps in a way that resonated with both technical and nontechnical audiences. The following year saw the release of another influential publication, *The DevOps Handbook* by Gene Kim, Jez Humble, Patrick Debois, and John Willis. This practical guide helped many organizations start their DevOps journey by providing a comprehensive framework for implementing DevOps.

In 2013, the initial Puppet Labs (now Puppet) "State of DevOps" report by Kim and Humble drew attention. The report didn't just focus on technical metrics; it highlighted the business benefits of DevOps adoption, demonstrating that organizations implementing the approach could ship code 30 times faster than their peers, with a 50% reduction in failures. This tied DevOps practices directly to the business outcomes that leaders care about. The book *Accelerate: The Science of Lean Software and DevOps* (IT Revolution) by Nicole Forsgren, Jez Humble, and Gene Kim explored this theme in greater detail.

The introduction of Platform-as-a-Service (PaaS) and Docker in 2013 marked another pivotal moment, as these technologies simplified the deployment and management of applications, making DevOps practices feasible on a larger scale. Prior to this, the complexity of managing infrastructure and applications made widespread adoption of DevOps challenging. The launch of AWS Lambda in 2014 further transformed the landscape by pioneering event-driven function execution at scale, allowing developers to focus on writing code without worrying about the underlying infrastructure. Meanwhile, Kubernetes, also introduced in 2014, provided a robust framework for orchestrating containerized applications at scale, ensuring that deployments were reliable, efficient, and scalable.

By the latter half of the decade, machine learning (ML) techniques began to creep into DevOps toolchains, especially in application performance monitoring (APM) and testing disciplines. Testing tools would use ML to optimize test execution and detect changes in user interfaces. Meanwhile, APM tools like Datadog and New Relic were early to brand themselves "AI Ops" as they used ML to identify problematic signals. By 2018, Harness applied ML to continuous delivery (*https://oreil.ly/4BH7E*) to detect problematic signals, enabling the system to identify when deployments caused issues and trigger necessary rollbacks. Together, these technologies laid the groundwork for modern DevOps by providing the necessary tools and frameworks to manage complex software systems efficiently, paving the way for AI-native DevOps.

DevOps 1.0

DevOps has progressed from a loose, niche concept to a well-established set of ideas we can refer to as "DevOps 1.0." Its attributes include:

Cultural transformation
> Recognizing the significance of cultural shifts to align software development and operations teams

Automation practices
> Implementing practices such as continuous integration and continuous delivery to streamline software delivery

Tools for automation
> Utilizing specific tools to automate various stages of the software delivery pipeline, including code commits, testing, deployment, provisioning, and production monitoring

Early adopters of DevOps 1.0 practices experienced immediate wins. In the early 2010s, many engineering teams were releasing software on a quarterly basis, with weeks of effort dedicated to manual testing, coordination, and production deployment. These release processes were slow, error-prone, and required off-hours scheduling to minimize risk. As organizations began embracing early DevOps principles—bringing development and operations teams closer together and automating key parts of the delivery pipeline—they achieved faster release cycles, greater reliability, and reduced manual effort. For many, the shift enabled a move from quarterly to biweekly or even weekly releases, setting the stage for more iterative development and faster time-to-value.

Challenges to DevOps 1.0

DevOps 1.0 provided valuable concepts, practices, and tools. However, companies today face new challenges in fully realizing the benefits of DevOps as a result of:

- Software trends that have introduced complexities that require DevOps to adapt
- DevOps 1.0 toolsets that either are lacking in features or have become overly complex for many organizations

The following sections will explore the details of these challenges.

The adoption of cloud-native and microservices architectures.   New architecture patterns involve dozens of discrete microservices deployed to individual containers. DevOps 1.0 pipelines were not equipped to address the requirements of these new architectures.

Over the past decade, microservice and cloud-native architectures have become the de facto standard for modern software development, driven by the need for greater scalability, flexibility, and agility in software systems. These architectures introduce significant new requirements for DevOps teams. The adoption of microservices leads to a proliferation of services to deploy, each with its own dependencies and configurations. Orchestrating deployments and maintaining consistency across these distributed services becomes increasingly challenging.

The usage of containers (a key feature of cloud-native systems) and serverless architectures necessitates new strategies for deployment and management and adds another layer of complexity. DevOps teams must now handle deployments across dozens or even hundreds of ephemeral containers or serverless functions, requiring robust orchestration tools, automated processes for building and managing container lifecycles, and a deep understanding of these emerging technologies. Automating the entire lifecycle of containers—from building images, to pushing them to registries, to rolling out updates with minimal downtime—is critical for efficient container management.

The rise of open source software. Open source software (OSS) has become a ubiquitous part of modern software development. While OSS offers numerous benefits, it introduces new challenges for DevOps teams. Managing dependencies, ensuring compatibility with different versions, and maintaining security patches across multiple OSS components can be a daunting task. Additionally, teams must carefully vet the code and ensure it aligns with their organization's security and compliance standards.

The importance of the digital experience and consumerization of enterprise. In this era of digital disruption, Marc Andreessen's prophetic claim that software is eating the world proves ever more accurate. The digital experience a company provides is becoming the primary touchpoint for customers, shaping how they experience a brand. Moreover, the consumerization of enterprise technology means that employees expect the same seamless experiences and continual updates they get with customer-targeted applications. These expectations pressure DevOps teams to deliver even more frequent releases, maintain high availability, and enable experimentation to power rapid innovation.

Outgrowing DevOps 1.0 toolsets

In the years since the first DevOpsDays in 2009, what we need from our tools has changed. Delivery cadences have accelerated while regulatory burdens have increased. Take artifact registries: originally introduced as local caches to speed up builds, they're now essential for securing software supply chains across a multitude of languages. To simplify deployments, we containerized and our builds became longer, making our continuous integration builds anything but continuous. We shifted from one set of configuration management tools to newer, cloud-native declarative tools.

But we still need to test, secure, and govern those infrastructure changes. Meanwhile, new tools arrive all the time—each promising improvements but also requiring wiring up to everything else. For many teams, the current stack is crumbling.

Pipelines quickly become very complex. Organizations are managing an average of 10 or more different tools to deploy software. For example, an automation pipeline to deploy Rails, Sidekiq, and NodeJS apps might include the following tools:

- GitHub actions for running CI
- Libraries for instrumenting Sidekiq, Rails, and Puma and pushing application metrics into Prometheus
- Docker image building and Kubernetes
- Artifactory for storing images and Helm charts
- ArgoCD for GitOps deployments on Kubernetes
- Helm for managing deployments and upgrades
- Terraform for managing the Amazon Web Services (AWS) infrastructure, roles, permissions, etc.
- New Relic for exception capture and monitoring
- Kube-state-metrics for gathering container metrics
- Prometheus for storing metrics
- Grafana for making Prometheus metrics consumable

The integration and management of this toolset may pose a considerable challenge for a team with limited resources. Let's look at some of the challenges of a DIY approach.

Widely used open source tools are often suboptimal.   A DIY approach to DevOps often results in a less efficient pipeline. Some open source tools lack features that could reduce developer effort and shorten the time to production. For example, maintaining uptime and scaling in Jenkins requires significant resources. Long testing times can lead to slow builds. Lastly, the model for reusing pipelines is copy/paste, leading to "pipeline sprawl," which can be difficult and expensive to maintain. Chapter 3 will cover these issues in additional detail.

DIY pipelines result in redundant and wasteful efforts.   Often teams must implement plumbing to bring tools and systems together. This leads to substantial reinventing of the wheel. For example, Jenkins and ArgoCD are common tools used for CI/CD. These tools provide powerful features for automating the software development and deployment process, but they require teams to build essential constructs like role-based access control (RBAC), audit logs, and notifications from scratch.

Implementing and maintaining is an effort that could otherwise be applied to delivering value to customers.

Automation is often incomplete, requiring manual steps. A team using automated scripts for most of the deployment but requiring manual intervention to configure environment variables can lead to inconsistent deployments if not all team members follow the same procedure. Incomplete automation can lead to gaps in monitoring and feedback loops, as manual steps might not trigger automated alerts or metrics collection. Manual steps introduce the risk of human error, which can lead to downtime or security breaches. Thus, incomplete automation in DevOps can lead to inefficiencies, errors, and scalability issues.

Governance is an afterthought. Without up-front governance, teams might overlook compliance requirements (such as meeting General Data Protection Regulation [GDPR] standards), leading to costly rework or fines when issues are discovered later. If security measures are applied inconsistently or as an afterthought, applications are left vulnerable to attacks. Without clear governance policies, resources such as cloud services or infrastructure might be overprovisioned or underutilized, leading to wasted costs (a topic we'll cover in Chapter 9). Without oversight, teams may use different tools, processes, and standards, leading to integration challenges and inefficiencies.

DevOps 2.0

DevOps 1.0 has significantly accelerated the software delivery process for many companies. Yet its complexity, the gaps it leaves, and the investment it requires create room for improvement. Enter what we're calling DevOps 2.0—a vision defined by a simpler developer experience, end-to-end automation with views to easily manage all of the moving parts, and AI capabilities that augment the entire pipeline. This evolution shifts the focus from tools and processes to the people and outcomes they serve.

DevOps 2.0 processes and tools enhance the developer experience with powerful new features. Developers start new projects and services within minutes by automating the setup of development and delivery toolchains. Out-of-the-box integrations give teams the ability to easily spin up and connect repositories, agile projects, and pipelines. To streamline the process further, templates encapsulate an organization's best practices, ensuring consistency and eliminating work management overhead when creating new services. Teams focus on building their applications, not on tedious infrastructure setup. AI agents perform increasingly complex DevOps tasks, such as automatically diagnosing and resolving infrastructure and pipeline issues, optimizing resource allocation, and suggesting architectural improvements based on observed performance patterns.

DevOps 2.0 tools detangle the complexity of DevOps 1.0 solutions with a more cohesive, tightly integrated toolset. Essential constructs (RBAC, audit logs) are integrated. Support for various deployment strategies and experimentation approaches are built in, enabling the frequent releases and rapid iterations teams need. New tools scale to support large-scale deployments across multiple environments, including on-premises, cloud, and hybrid setups. DevOps 2.0 tools will offer secure pipelines and policy enforcement to minimize the inherent risks of open source adoption and AI-written code.

Lastly, AI is being baked into DevOps 2.0 tools and processes throughout the software delivery pipeline. Emerging protocols like the Agent Control Protocol (ACP), Model Context Protocol (MCP), and Agent-to-Agent Protocol are helping enable seamless interaction between AI models and the broader ecosystem of tools, systems, and data. These protocols define standardized ways for AI agents to interact with tools, access data securely, and perform tasks within guardrails—enabling more dynamic and autonomous workflows.

In modern DevOps environments, the protocols act as bridges between AI capabilities and the operational infrastructure, allowing AI to do more than just observe and suggest; they empower it to take meaningful action while remaining auditable and compliant. As DevOps 2.0 embraces increasingly intelligent automation, these protocols provide the foundation for safe, scalable, and effective AI-driven operations that supercharge developer workflows. Imagine tools that can generate code, comments, tests, and infrastructure scripts, or pull out relevant code snippets using natural language search. In addition, ML speeds up test cycles by only executing relevant tests.

Leveraging AI, the tools provide personalized guidance during onboarding, detect vulnerabilities and offer remediation advice or instigate repairs, and even help write and understand policies. The reliability of deployments is improved through the analysis of observability telemetry to identify when rollbacks are needed. AI analyzes feature experiments to understand the impacts of change. This AI-driven transformation across the software development lifecycle (SDLC) is boosting productivity, improving quality, reducing risk, and enhancing the overall developer experience.

As developers can code increasingly quickly with AI coding assistants, a business's ability to quickly and safely deliver changes to production and understand if those changes have been beneficial will be the limiting factor to innovation. To do this well will require both doing the basics of DevOps well and infusing cutting-edge AI throughout every stage of delivery.

Summary

Modern software delivery emphasizes rapid releases, seamless experiences, and constant innovation, driving a need to transform traditional DevOps practices. While DevOps 1.0 laid the groundwork with CI/CD and initial cross-team collaboration, its reliance on complex toolchains built from disparate solutions creates hurdles. These challenges stem from the growing architectural complexity of applications (microservices, containers), the proliferation of open source components, and the need to manage increasingly diverse toolsets. DevOps 2.0 aims to address these issues by simplifying the developer experience, offering more integrated and intelligent toolsets, and infusing AI natively throughout the pipeline. This evolution promises greater efficiency, enhanced quality, and a focus on delivering value rather than just managing tools.

In addition, AI-native software delivery replaces static automation with autonomous agents (e.g., Code, DevOps, Security) to enable self-optimizing systems and proactive and unified ecosystems. It accelerates development velocity, enhances reliability, ensures compliance, reduces costs, and fosters scalable collaboration through autonomous code generation, contextual pipeline creation, predictive failure resolution, and real-time decision-making. While this is transformative, organizations must address AI governance, data privacy, and skill gaps to fully leverage its benefits.

In Chapters 2, 3, and 4, we will cover the backbone of DevOps automation. This includes source control management for effective version control, building and testing using continuous integration for efficient development, and deploying internally using continuous delivery systems for seamless software releases. We will explore both the DevOps 1.0 approaches and the opportunities presented by DevOps 2.0.

CHAPTER 2

Source Control Management

Imagine a scenario where you and your team are collaborating on a complex software project. Multiple minds are contributing, making revisions and enhancements. Without a clear system for managing changes, you risk overwriting each other's work and losing track of who updated what and why they made those changes. Without a clear system to tag sets of changes, you are unable to navigate back to a previous stable version of your team's code should an issue arise. Without defined workflows and structured access control, anyone can change anything at any time, with no oversight. Without controls, your team is unable to determine which code files were used to build a particular release should you need to recreate it.

Next, imagine that several teams have worked for months on a new application and it is now nearing time to deploy to your production environment. Ad hoc fixes and tweaks have been made to various development and QA environments, but those have not been reliably reflected in the production environment. Important production settings have not been repeated in QA environments, and development environments vary widely. Given the increasing complexity of the required environments, spinning up new environments has become a time-consuming and error-prone bottleneck that creates frustration and delay.

These situations are recipes for dysfunction and wasted effort. Source control management (SCM) practices were created to address these very problems. At its core, SCM is about tracking and managing changes made to code and other critical resources like configurations over time.

Today, artificial intelligence is transforming how we approach SCM. AI can automatically detect risky changes, suggest improvements to code or configurations, and even help resolve merge conflicts by understanding the intent behind modifications. It can identify inconsistencies across environments, recommend corrections, and optimize deployment workflows. AI-powered tools are not just helping teams manage complexity—they're enabling faster, safer, and more resilient development cycles. As software delivery becomes more distributed and dynamic, AI is becoming an essential partner in making SCM more intelligent, proactive, and efficient.

Introducing Source Control Management

The problem of coordinating changes across a team dates back to the early days of programming, and the history of SCM practices is intricately linked to the evolution of computer programming. In this section we'll explore how SCM has evolved and the critical role AI tools play in modern SCM.

A Short History of Source Control Management

In the early days of programming, programs were relatively simple; they were constrained by limited hardware, and code management was rudimentary. As CPUs became powerful and sophisticated, computation and code became more complex. Code repositories, central stores that provide basic SCM functions, first emerged in the 1970s alongside the rise of high-level languages and structured programming methodologies. Tools like Source Code Control System (SCCS) offered basic version tracking, allowing developers to revert to previous versions and see the history of changes. These early systems mirrored the shift toward more organized program development.

SCM further evolved in the 1970s with the emergence of more structured software engineering teams. Tools like Revision Control System (RCS), introduced in 1982, and Concurrent Versions System (CVS), introduced in 1986, added features crucial for collaboration, including branching. This enabled more complex project management and a collaborative culture.

In the early 1990s, IBM Rational ClearCase emerged as a commercial solution for SCM. It emphasized robust configuration management and process customization, making it suitable for complex software development environments. Subversion (SVN), developed by CollabNet, is another centralized code repository that gained popularity. SVN 1.0 was released in 2004 to address shortcomings in CVS and provide missing features.

Distributed version control and Git

The rise of Agile methodologies and open source in the early 2000s put new demands on software development. Rapid releases meant that teams required more flexibility and control over increasingly complex codebases. Teams themselves changed, becoming larger and often geographically dispersed. Git was created in 2005 by Linus Torvalds, the creator of the Linux kernel. He needed a powerful and efficient system to manage the massive codebase of the Linux project, and existing options fell short.

A version control system (VCS) is the core technology that tracks changes to files over time, forming the foundation of any SCM approach. Unlike most earlier code repositories, Git is a distributed VCS. With a centralized VCS, everyone works from a single copy of the codebase stored in a central server (repository). Each developer has their own local copy (working copy) that they can modify. When a developer makes changes and commits them, those changes are immediately uploaded to the central repository, making them visible to everyone else. To see the latest changes from others, developers simply need to update their local copy from the central repository. Figure 2-1 shows a centralized VCS.

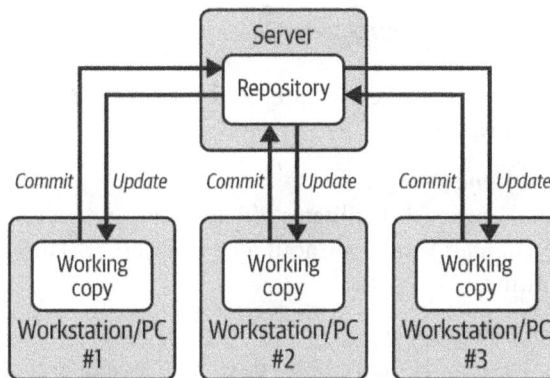

Figure 2-1. Centralized version control (https://oreil.ly/YLeDg)

Distributed systems take a different approach. Here, each developer has a complete copy of the codebase (including both the repository and their working copy) on their local machine. Changes made by a developer are private to their local copy until they explicitly share them with the team. This is done by "pushing" their changes to the central repository. Similarly, to see updates made by other developers, users need to download ("fetch") those changes from the central repository into their local copy. Figure 2-2 shows a Git distributed VCS.

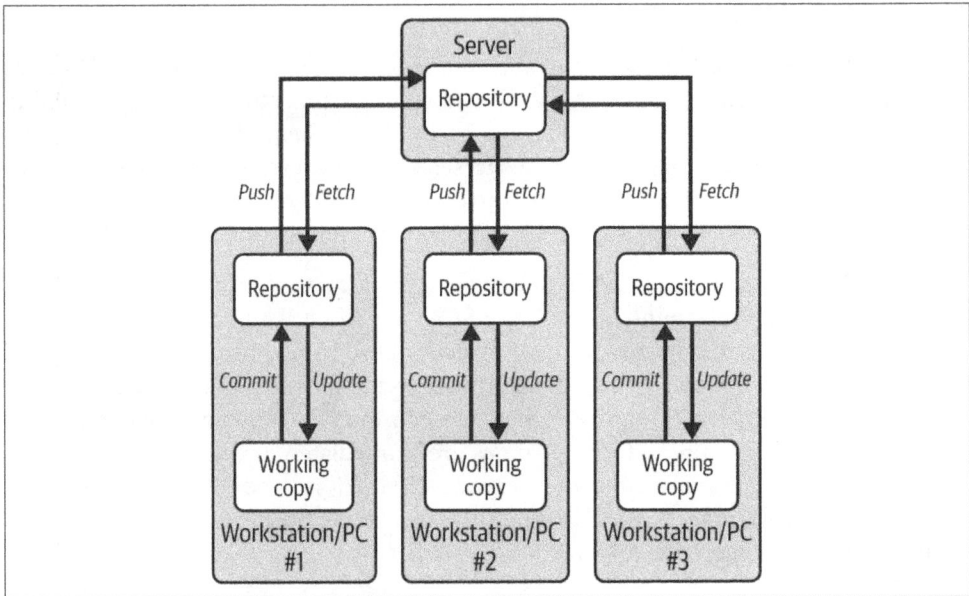

Figure 2-2. Distributed version control with Git

Git's focus on speed, its distributed nature, and robust branching made it a game-changer in a number of ways:

Distributed facilitates offline work

Git's decentralized approach facilitates efficient and independent work, as developers can make changes locally without a central server. This also enabled developers to work offline.

Flexible branching and merging

Git's branching system is incredibly flexible. Developers can create isolated branches to work on new features or bug fixes without affecting the main codebase. Merging these branches back into the main codebase is a smooth and efficient process. This empowers developers to experiment and iterate more freely.

Lightweight and efficient for large codebases

Git excels at handling large codebases efficiently. It only stores the differences between code versions, making it faster and requiring less storage space than traditional SCM systems.

Nonlinear history aids organizations

Unlike some SCM systems that enforce a linear history, Git allows developers to rewrite history through functionalities like rebasing. This flexibility helps maintain a clean and organized codebase.

The first widely used hosted Git repositories arrived a few years later. GitHub, the most popular today, was launched in 2008. These platforms are built upon the power of Git, offering a user-friendly web interface, cloud storage for codebases, and collaboration features. This combination transformed Git from a powerful but technical tool to an accessible and social platform for software development, making it a cornerstone of modern software development workflows.

While traditional centralized repositories still have a legacy footprint and are in use in environments with very specific needs, Git is now the predominant choice. A 2022 Stack Overflow survey (*https://oreil.ly/rLVE0*) found that 94% of overall respondents used Git and 98% of those using any source control use Git. For this reason, we will focus our attention on Git repository variations.

Branching out with Git

In 2010, Gitflow branching conventions emerged to use branching to provide a clear separation between development, feature creation, and release preparation. Figure 2-3 shows a Gitflow workflow.

In the Gitflow workflow:

1. The main codebase resides on a branch called "main." This branch is typically considered stable and should only contain production-ready code.

2. A new "develop" branch, which serves as the continuous integration branch for all development work, is created.

3. Feature development happens on isolated branches (feature/release branches) that branch from the develop branch. Developers work on new features and bug fixes on these feature branches. Once a feature is complete and thoroughly tested, it's merged back into the develop branch.

4. The develop branch acts as an integration point for all completed features. It represents the upcoming release version and is continuously updated with merged feature branches.

5. When it's time for a release, a release branch is created from "develop." Bug fixes and minor adjustments can be made on this branch. Once finalized, the release branch is merged back into "main" to create the official release. A corresponding tag is created in "main" to mark the release version.

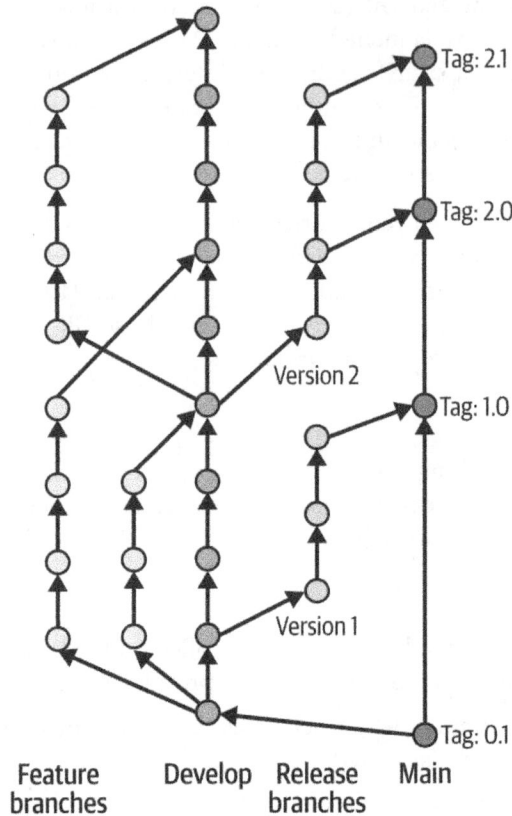

Figure 2-3. Gitflow workflow (https://oreil.ly/L2ZLg)

Pull requests, sometimes abbreviated as PRs, are a core collaboration feature in Git version control used for code review and integration, and are widely used with Gitflow and other branching models. Pull requests provide a structured way for developers to propose changes to a codebase and get them reviewed by others before merging them into the main branch.

Gitflow's emphasis on planned releases and separate release branches has been challenged by newer Git branching models. Fueled by the growing adoption of continuous integration and continuous delivery, these models prioritize faster deployments with more frequent updates. Trunk-based development discards the idea of a dedicated development branch altogether. Instead, features are continuously integrated directly into the main branch (often called "trunk" or "main") after rigorous testing. Figure 2-4 shows this pattern.

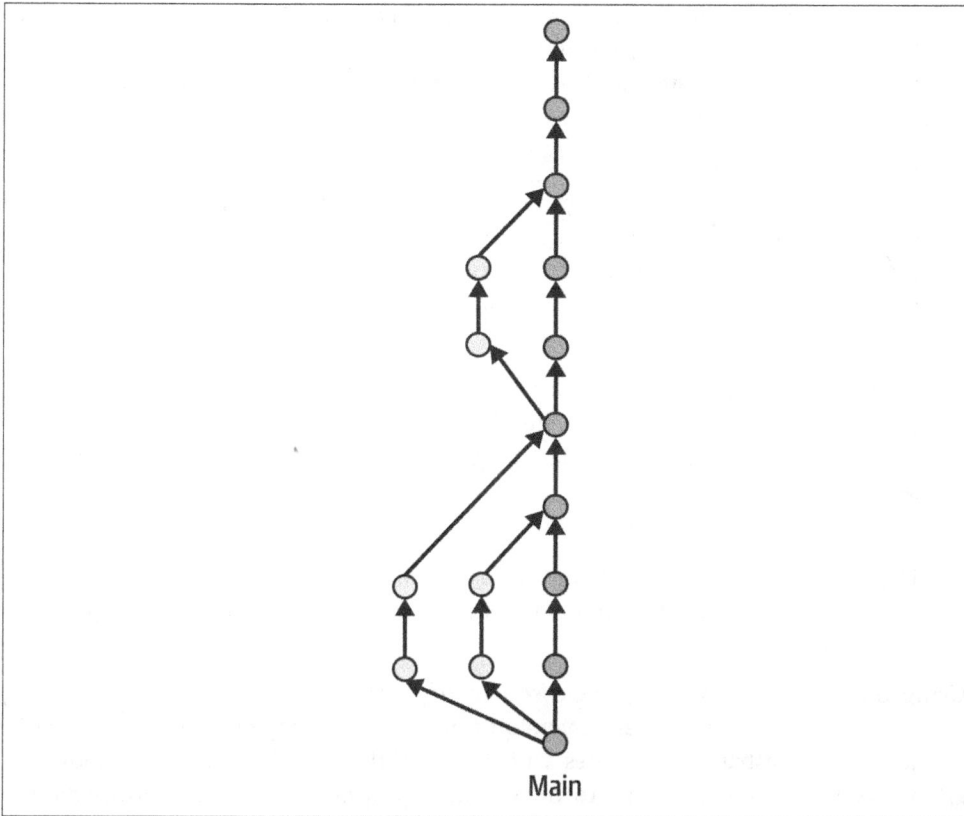

Main

Figure 2-4. Trunk-based development

This streamlined approach allows for quicker feedback loops and faster deployments, aligning well with modern DevOps practices. Pull requests remain essential in these workflows, ensuring code quality through code review before merging changes into the main branch.

GitOps and Source Control Management

We have seen how code repositories evolved alongside programming and software development practices to solve the problems we imagined, enabling teams to collaborate effectively in source code. But what about deployment problems? How can we efficiently and systematically produce the environments we need and how can we streamline the deployment of our code into the production environment?

Here is where GitOps comes in. In bringing Dev and Ops together, DevOps empha-sizes the importance of automation in eliminating manual errors and helps ensure consistency across environments. This translates to faster deployments, improved reliability, and reduced risk. GitOps refers to automating the process of provisioning infrastructure, especially in modern container-first, cloud infrastructures. GitOps emphasizes the use of a code repository (usually Git) as the single source of truth for the desired state of the system and leverages automation to continuously reconcile the actual state with the desired state. Resources stored to our repositories can include:

Infrastructure configuration
> Files that define components needed for the environment, the type and number of virtual machines (VMs), storage configurations, network settings, and security policies. This can include declarative and imperative configurations and deployment scripts.

Environment variables
> These are essential for storing sensitive information like passwords or API keys that should not be directly embedded in code. Infrastructure as Code (IaC) tools often have mechanisms for managing and referencing environment variables securely.

Additional resources
> Depending on the complexity of the environment, the repository might also store other resources such as container images (through git-lfs) used for application deployment.

Using our repository as that single source of truth, we can take advantage of its powerful features. We get detailed version tracking and change histories, and we can manage our infrastructure updates with Git workflows that promote collaboration and oversight like code reviews through pull requests. Well-managed infrastructure automation translates to faster deployments, fewer errors, and reliable environments every time a new one needs to be created. We'll learn more about using GitOps to deploy in Chapter 4.

Monorepos and Remote Caching

We mentioned the importance of microservices in Chapter 1. Two key practices that enhance productivity in microservices-based systems are the use of monorepos and remote caching.

A monorepo (monolithic repository) is a single version-controlled code repository that stores the code for multiple projects or services. In a microservices context, this approach simplifies collaboration, streamlines dependency management, enables atomic updates across services, and reduces versioning conflicts.

Remote caching refers to storing build artifacts—such as compiled code or test results—on remote servers. Tools like Nx use this technique to significantly speed up development workflows by allowing teams to reuse previously generated outputs instead of rebuilding from scratch, reducing redundant computations.

Together, monorepos and remote caching support faster and more efficient CI/CD pipelines and contribute to improved overall system performance. However, monorepos can introduce complexity as projects scale, and remote caching can raise concerns about vendor lock-in if not thoughtfully implemented.

AI in Source Control Management

AI tools have revolutionized how developers approach coding. GitHub Copilot, Cursor, Harness AI Code Agent, and similar coding assistants/agents act as intelligent pair programmers, offering real-time code suggestions based on project context. These tools can predict and suggest entire lines or blocks of code, significantly speeding up the development process.

Beyond code completion, AI assistants can:

- Generate boilerplate code structures automatically
- Suggest different implementation approaches
- Provide code explanation and documentation
- Assist with debugging and optimization

AI-native software delivery starts with an AI-native SCM. The integration of AI with SCM extends beyond just code completion. Within SCMs, AI can analyze repository patterns, identify potential bugs before they reach production, and suggest architectural improvements based on best practices observed across similar projects. This proactive approach significantly reduces technical debt and improves code quality from the earliest stages of development. We will explore some of these themes later in the chapter.

In the following sections we'll walk through how SCM systems fit into the delivery pipeline. With that understanding, we'll discuss factors to consider when choosing an SCM that is right for your team. Lastly, we'll look at characteristics of modern code repositories, including the role of AI, that can simplify your entire software development pipeline.

Source Control Management in the Delivery Pipeline

The core repository is a critical component of the delivery pipeline, anchoring the entire pipeline process. It serves as the single source of truth for the code, ensuring consistency and reliability, and it is the entity that developers interact with continually, initiating integration and delivery activities.

Figure 2-5 depicts the relationship of the code repository to continuous integration and delivery.

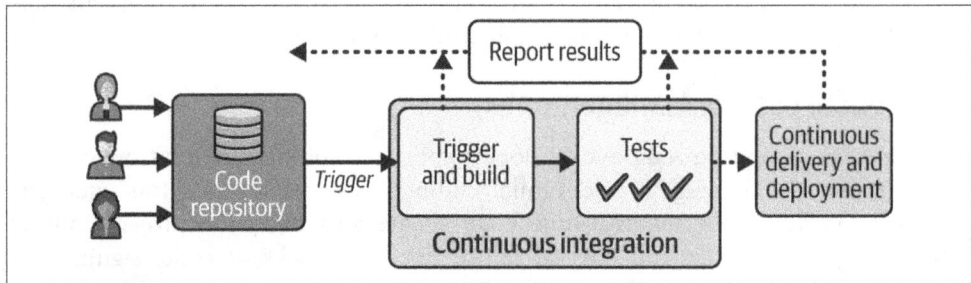

Figure 2-5. Developer actions against the code repository instigate the CI/CD pipeline

Let's walk through the three main parts of a typical pipeline:

Code repository
> Developers work against the code repository, committing changes and opening and closing pull requests.

Continuous integration
> Continuous integration is initiated by specific actions within a code repository. These triggers can be customized, including events such as code commits, the opening or closing of pull requests, or other relevant actions determined by your team's specific needs and practices. CI gives developers rapid feedback on code changes. By automating builds and tests, CI acts as an early warning system, alerting developers to potential bugs, integration issues, or even style violations. This immediate feedback empowers developers to quickly address problems, preventing them from snowballing into larger, more costly issues down the line. With CI, your codebase stays in a consistently deployable state, ready for the next step in your delivery pipeline.

Continuous delivery and deployment
> Continuous delivery and deployment steps automate the provisioning of infrastructure and the deployment of new code versions to one or more pre-production environments. Various types of tests are typically executed against the app running in pre-production environments. We'll look at these steps in Chapter 4. Finally, automatic or manual decisions gate the final deployment of the software into the production environment. We'll discuss these steps at length in Chapter 8. By deploying smaller changes frequently, CD streamlines the delivery process, reduces release risk, and enhances the ability to respond to user feedback quickly.

Many code repositories build in secret detection features. Secrets can include the following:

API keys
    Unique identifiers used to authenticate and authorize access to various web services and APIs

Access tokens
    Temporary credentials that grant specific access rights to an application or resource

OAuth tokens
    Tokens used for delegated authorization, allowing one application to access resources on behalf of a user

Private keys
    Secret keys used in asymmetric encryption to decrypt messages or verify digital signatures

Usernames and passwords
    Credentials used for basic authentication to systems and services

Database connection strings
    Details needed to establish a connection to a database, often including sensitive information like hostnames, usernames, and passwords

Cloud service connection strings
    Strings used to connect to cloud services like Azure Storage or AWS S3, potentially containing access keys and other secrets

Some code repositories will prevent or warn a developer when attempting to commit or merge code with a detected secret. CI processes can play a role in secret detection, preventing them from reaching a production environment. An ideal approach is to leverage both for comprehensive security.

Code Repository Considerations

Given the importance of SCM to software development, selecting a code repository is one of the first decisions a team will make. *Where will we put the source code?* is a question a team will need to answer to even kick off a project.

First and foremost, a repository must support the basic operations and the developer workflows that are critical to your team:

- Creating, importing, and cloning repositories with support for distributed offline work
- Branching, merging, and defining branching rules to meet your specific team's needs (e.g., limiting branch creation/deletion to specific users)
- Creating, reviewing, and merging pull requests, along with defining pull request policies in line with the governance your team requires (e.g., requiring all changes to be associated with a pull request, prohibiting direct commits, or setting a minimum number of required reviewer approvals)
- Creating and modifying tags, and defining tag policies (e.g., enforcing tag names to adhere to a specific pattern like semantic versioning)

While there may be differences in the implementation details, these are expected repository features.

In creating a delivery pipeline, teams typically start with repository choice first; because this is a choice that can have far-reaching effects on the implementation, it is critical to ensure your code repository will support seamless integration within a broader ecosystem. Your code repository should function in an ecosystem that enhances your team's productivity instead of adding to their workload. In addition, a solution should be cost-effective and provide the transparency your organization requires.

Comprehensive Integrations

A well-designed DevOps ecosystem is characterized by easy-to-use tooling and comprehensive integrations with the functions and services that your delivery pipeline requires. This stands in contrast to a piecemeal approach, where developers are burdened with manual integration of many disparate tools, which can lead to issues that are difficult to troubleshoot and security risks. It is also contrasted with overly complex single-platform solutions, often suffering from feature bloat, that are difficult to configure.

An example of streamlined integration is configuration-as-code. This practice allows updates to your delivery pipeline to be versioned and tracked directly within your repository, just like your project code. You can further enhance collaboration and governance by enforcing workflows that require changes to be made through pull requests and approvals, mirroring standard development practices.

Another feature example relates to security/vulnerability scanning. Displaying detected vulnerabilities and suggested remediations in the context of a pull request helps the developer quickly understand and resolve any detected issue.

AI-Powered Features

The past few years have seen explosive growth in coding assistants or agents that use large language models to improve developer efficiency. These coding assistants help with auto-completing code, generating code suggestions, understanding what a piece of code does, and many other use cases. When AI assistants are integrated with code repositories to have access to the full codebase as context—not just isolated code snippets—they can generate more accurate and relevant suggestions.

MCP plays a key role here by providing a universal, standardized way to connect AI models and code assistants with various data sources, including repositories like Harness Code Repository, GitHub, and Git. This eliminates the need for custom integrations, reducing development effort and increasing efficiency.

Another powerful application of generative AI (GenAI) in code repositories is semantic search—the ability to search an entire codebase using natural language. Tools like Sourcegraph's Cody and Harness Code Repository enable developers to ask questions like, "How is authentication implemented and where is this code?" rather than relying on keyword-based searches like "log in" or "authenticate." This capability is especially valuable for onboarding new team members and helping them quickly understand complex codebases without deep familiarity with project-specific terminology.

Regarding code reviews, tools like DeepCode and Codacy use ML algorithms to review code changes, automatically detecting potential bugs, code smells, and adherence to coding standards more efficiently than manual reviews. Other use cases for AI in SCMs are enhancing security by automatically scanning for vulnerabilities and compliance issues before code is committed and recommending fixes for those issues, summarizing pull requests, and generating software delivery pipelines using SCM as one of the data sources.

It is important to note that with AI systems, results depend heavily on the data used to train the AI models. So, for example, "good" code will result in good code suggestions and reviews, and "bad" code will result in bad code suggestions and reviews.

Measuring the impact of AI is equally important in verifying whether using AI has actually had a positive impact on the developers. Tools such as Harness Software Engineering Insights and others can help with measuring the productivity of developers using different coding assistants and also compare them with the developers that don't use any coding assistants.

AI-powered SCMs accelerate time-to-market by generating fast and reliable code (especially when well-trained), improving code quality by identifying issues—including security vulnerabilities—at the source, and enhancing team collaboration by elevating the quality and efficiency of code reviews.

Efficiency and Transparency Through Open Source

Whether or not your DevOps tools are open source is an important consideration. Open source solutions can be cost-effective for organizations with budget constraints, and the transparency they offer has advantages as well.

Proprietary solutions can often claim to offer reliable uptime and dedicated customer support teams to address any technical issues you encounter. However, there are often subscription fees for enterprise users, which can be a significant cost factor for small teams. Open source codebases are free to use, making them ideal for teams with limited budgets. The open source nature allows for transparency and community-driven development. Developers have access to the source code, enabling customization of the platform to fit specific needs. However, they often have to rely on the community for troubleshooting and support. While valuable, open source may not offer the same level of guaranteed assistance as a commercial provider. In addition, while open source promotes transparency, it also means potential vulnerabilities are publicly visible.

Open core solutions, like Harness.io and GitLab, provide a middle ground. They offer a free, feature-limited version, akin to open source.

Lastly, OSS can be put into escrow if needed for regulatory requirements or to ensure continuity of business generally. This provides assurance that in the event the tool provider goes out of business you will still have access to the tools needed to build, test, and monitor your application and to recreate your development, testing, and production environments.

A Platform Approach

Traditional, piecemeal DevOps toolchains often create data silos and hinder visibility into the entire SDLC. However, a single DevOps platform offers a compelling solution by providing end-to-end visibility. For example, it enables tracking of every change, from the initial commit in the code repository to the final deployment on production servers. This holistic view helps you to identify bottlenecks, pinpoint potential issues early in the development cycle, and measure the overall effectiveness of your DevOps practices. Furthermore, comprehensive audit trails provide a clear record of all activity, simplifying troubleshooting and ensuring compliance with security regulations.

A unified platform also streamlines governance and unlocks the potential for intelligent automation. Managing governance policies across disparate tools can be cumbersome and error-prone. A single platform allows you to define and enforce policies consistently throughout your entire development pipeline. This ensures code adheres to coding standards, security best practices, and internal guidelines. For example, you can streamline governance by implementing a policy such as *scan code before committing, during the CI process, and during the CD process using (your organization's) approved security scanner.* With a unified platform this can be easily implemented as a template that gets reused.

Additionally, with a complete understanding of the deployment context, including infrastructure and configuration details, the platform can offer intelligent code suggestions that optimize performance and efficiency. Imagine an AI-powered assistant that recommends code tweaks based on how the service will be deployed, potentially saving development time and improving code quality.

Access Control, an Example

As teams assemble a delivery toolchain, it's common to start with individual point solutions. However, this piecemeal approach can lead to significant operational overhead. In this section, we'll look at the example of RBAC to see how a cohesive delivery pipeline can simplify operations and empower development teams.

Most collaboration tools use role-based access to functionality in some form or another. Code repositories will support built-in roles, or will include built-in roles and will allow users to define custom roles. GitHub, for example, defines the roles *Read, Triage, Write, Maintain,* and *Admin.* These roles correspond to levels of access; the Read role is recommended for noncode contributors, whereas the Admin role is designed for users who require full access to the project, including sensitive and destructive actions.

These systems use RBAC, a method of managing access to resources within a system that centers on three core elements, namely users, roles, and permissions:

- Users represent individuals or accounts requiring access.
- Roles are defined sets of permissions that grant access to specific resources or actions within the system.
- Permissions are the fundamental units of control, defining what actions a user can take (like reading, editing, or deleting data).

Users are not directly assigned permissions. Instead, they are assigned one or more roles. Once a user is assigned a role, they inherit all the permissions associated with that role. This approach simplifies access management by eliminating the need to individually assign permissions to every user. Instead, permissions are defined at the role level, and users are granted access based on the roles they are assigned. Figure 2-6 illustrates users assigned to roles and the sets of permissions associated with roles.

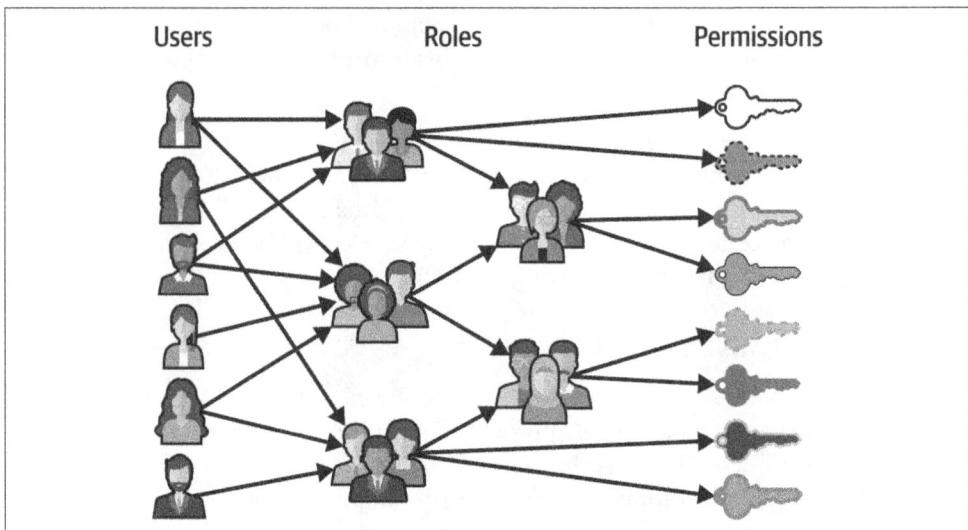

Figure 2-6. Users are assigned to roles; permissions are associated with roles

Using role-based access is a common pattern that reduces administrative and enhances security by enforcing the principle of least privilege—users are granted only the permissions necessary for their job functions. Role-based access also helps with compliance, as it provides clear documentation of who has access to what within the system.

Defining Roles, a Platform Approach

Imagine a DevOps ecosystem consisting of a Git repo, Jenkins, Terraform to manage an AWS infrastructure, Ansible for configuration management, and Datadog to capture performance metrics. In a system like this, constructed of several disparate tools, you might find that you need to define similar roles in each system, and repeatedly add the same. Provisioning a new developer might take several time-consuming steps. Let's look at how an all-in-one platform handles RBAC using a platform approach.

As an example, the Harness Platform has a three-level hierarchical structure. The three levels, or scopes, are Account, Organization (Org), and Project:

- Account is the topmost entity. It can exercise control and has visibility over the entire platform.

- Organization is a unit of control where people and projects from the same business unit can be organized in an independent hierarchy. An organization can have multiple projects.

- Projects represent the basic unit of collaboration in which users are grouped together to work on the same task.

Resource Groups are an RBAC component that define the objects that a user can access. Objects are any Harness resource, including projects, pipelines, connectors, secrets, delegates, environments, users, and more. When you assign a Resource Group to a user, the access defined in the Resource Group is granted to the target user. Resource Groups can be defined at any scope.

Roles likewise can be defined at each scope. Roles are applied together to Resource Groups to create a complete set of permissions and access. For example, you can assign the Pipeline Executor role to a Resource Group that only allows access to specific pipelines, rather than all pipelines in the project.

Summary

In this chapter, we introduced SCM, a cornerstone of modern software development. SCM addresses the challenges of team collaboration and managing changes to code-bases over time. It enables teams to collaborate effectively and manage code changes over time.

SCM is essential to DevOps and CI/CD workflows, and its role is expanding with the emergence of AI-native SCM systems. These intelligent systems can generate, review, analyze, and optimize code, transforming how teams write and manage software. By automating routine tasks, enhancing accuracy, and surfacing insights, AI-powered SCM systems accelerate development and improve delivery efficiency.

We also discussed the importance of selecting the right code repository and the benefits of a unified DevOps platform for cohesive workflows and stronger governance. With a solid SCM foundation in place, Chapter 3 dives into how continuous integration automates builds and unit tests to ensure code quality and development speed.

The Build and Pre-Deployment Testing Steps of Continuous Integration

Simply put, our modern software delivery practices provide a structure to help us plan, write, build, test, and deploy software. In Chapter 2, we looked at how SCM systems help track and manage changes as we write code.

In this chapter, we turn our attention to continuous integration. Figure 3-1 shows a CI/CD pipeline that we'll look at shortly and return to in Chapters 4 and 8.

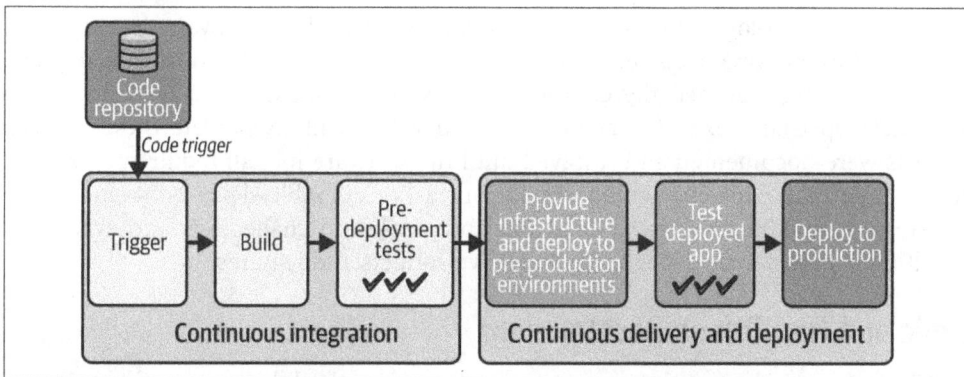

Figure 3-1. A CI/CD pipeline

We'll explore the continuous integration pipeline with emphasis on build processes and pre-deployment testing (static scans, unit tests, and integration tests). We'll demonstrate how an AI-native approach can accelerate CI through GenAI, agentic AI, and open standards such as MCP implementations. These technologies enable automated processes, predictive optimization, standardized context management, and intelligent testing strategies throughout the build, cache, and testing phases.

In addition to the key continuous integration steps, we'll review continuous integration tools and discuss factors to consider when selecting one. You will come away with an understanding of how to improve efficiency, quality, and security in your build pipeline.

A Short History of Building and Testing Software

This is a familiar story. In 1947, while working on the Harvard Mark II computer, a team of engineers discovered a moth trapped in a relay, causing the machine to malfunction. They removed the moth and taped it into their logbook with the note "First actual case of bug being found," thus solidifying the association of "bug" with software errors. Finding the bug in the machine accurately characterizes testing in the early days of software development. Developers would write code independently and integrate it. Testing was typically done manually and ad hoc. Teams focused on finding the bugs, ridding machines of "the moths" when errors were discovered. Bugs were typically found in production, resulting in delays and unreliable software.

As software development evolved, testing became more formalized and rigorous, with a focus on trying to "break" the software to uncover defects. Formal testing methodologies and standards began to emerge, such as the IEEE 829 Standard for Software and System Test Documentation (1983).

Structured Software Development and Waterfall Methodologies

Waterfall methodologies introduced a structured approach to software development, where testing became a distinct phase. Acceptance criteria, defined during requirements gathering, outlined the conditions the software must meet. Test cases were then developed and executed at the end of development to validate these criteria. Defects were documented and resolved until the software met all requirements. This formal approach, however, often resulted in a considerable delay between coding and testing, making early issue detection and resolution challenging and eventually resulting in a slower time-to-market for new products and features.

Agile and Test-Driven Development

In Chapter 1, we discussed the emergence of Agile methodologies in software development, motivated by the inefficiencies and limitations of the waterfall development. Agile methodologies' more flexible and responsive development model emphasized frequent feedback and iterative development, necessitating new testing approaches that could keep pace with the rapid development cycles. This led to new testing approaches.

Extreme Programming (XP), developed by Kent Beck, Ward Cunningham, and Ron Jeffries, was a specific Agile methodology defined by a set of best practices. One fundamental XP practice is test-driven development (TDD). In TDD, you write tests before writing the associated code. Beck's influential book *Extreme Programming Explained* (Addison-Wesley), first published in 1999, popularized TDD to a wide audience, and early tools like JUnit (for Java) and NUnit (for .NET) provided developers with frameworks to easily write these types of tests before writing corresponding code.

Writing tests before code encourages developers to think deeply about desired code behavior, leading to better design and fewer defects. While this concept existed previously, TDD's specific approach of writing failing tests first and then coding to pass them aligned well with Agile's focus on short cycles and frequent delivery of working software. This practice redefined the notion of completeness: *A feature isn't done when the code is working, but when the automated tests are complete and passing.*

The automated tests created during TDD provide a safety net, allowing developers to refactor code with confidence, knowing that any regressions will be quickly caught by the tests. This enables faster iteration and more frequent releases, which in turn allows for quicker feedback from customers and stakeholders. The tests themselves also serve as a form of documentation, clearly articulating the expected behavior of the system.

Enter Continuous Integration

As we introduced in Chapter 1, CI is the practice of automating the integration of code changes from multiple contributors into a shared repository, frequently triggering automated builds and tests to ensure the software remains in a working state. This complemented TDD.

The roots of CI (*https://oreil.ly/neqmf*) trace back to the 1990s. Grady Booch first coined the term "continuous integration" in 1991, but it was Kent Beck and Ron Jeffries who truly put it into practice while collaborating on a project in 1997. Their goal was to address the "integration hell" that arose from infrequent code merges, where conflicts and errors would pile up and become increasingly difficult to resolve.

Early CI systems were often custom-built and tailored to specific projects. One notable example was CruiseControl, created in 2001 by ThoughtWorks. It was one of the first open source CI servers, allowing teams to automate the building and testing of software with every code commit. However, it lacked a user-friendly interface and flexible job scheduling, leading to the development of Hudson in 2005 by Kohsuke Kawaguchi. Hudson quickly gained popularity due to its ease of use and powerful features.

In 2011, a dispute with Oracle led to Hudson being forked into Jenkins (*https://oreil.ly/MF9WD*), which has since become one of the most widely used tools for not only continuous integration, but also continuous delivery and deployment.

The popularity of Jenkins can be attributed to its flexibility, extensibility, and vast plug-in ecosystem, allowing it to integrate with various tools and adapt to different workflows.

Continuous Integration Today

Continuous integration has evolved into a foundational practice in modern software development, and CI/CD systems are the backbone of any delivery pipeline. Through the continuous integration of code changes, teams have come to depend on the following advantages:

Reduced integration problems
> CI eliminates the dreaded "integration hell" by ensuring developers merge their code changes frequently, minimizing conflicts and making them easier to resolve.

Faster feedback
> CI's automated build and test processes provide developers with rapid feedback on their code changes, allowing them to catch and fix errors quickly, thus maintaining a stable and deployable codebase.

Increased efficiency and reliability
> By automating the build and testing process, CI eliminates manual errors and inconsistencies, leading to more reliable and predictable builds.

Improved transparency
> CI dashboards and notifications provide real-time visibility into the build and test status, allowing everyone on the team to track progress, identify potential issues, and collaborate more effectively.

Accelerated releases
> By streamlining and automating the build, test, and integration processes, CI enables faster and more frequent releases, allowing businesses to respond more rapidly to customer feedback and market changes.

In "Continuous Integration in the CI/CD Pipeline", we'll look at the function of CI in the delivery pipeline and explore the landscape of CI tools.

Continuous Integration in the CI/CD Pipeline

In Chapter 2, we introduced a CI/CD pipeline, focusing on the relationship between the code repository and code integration. Let's return to this pipeline and focus on the continuous integration, that is, the build step and the steps to execute pre-deployment test types, including static analysis, unit tests, and integration tests.

The pipeline in Figure 3-2 shows a typical CI process.

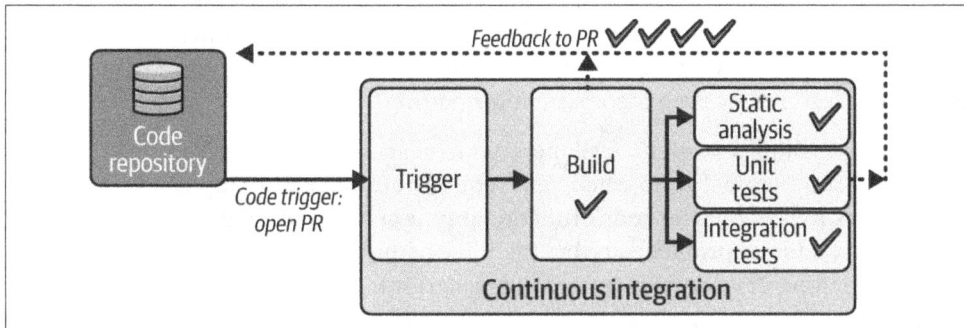

Figure 3-2. CI pipeline triggered by opening a Git PR

This example is triggered when a developer opens a pull request. The goal of this pipeline is to validate the changes proposed in the PR *before the changes are merged into the main branch*. Let's go through the steps:

1. Code trigger

A developer or an AI agent opens a pull request on the hosted repository (e.g., GitHub, GitLab, Bitbucket), which triggers the pipeline.

2. Checkout

The pipeline checks out the source code from the branch specified in the PR.

3. Build

The code is compiled (if necessary) and built into an executable or deployable artifact.

4. Static analysis

Tools like linters and code analyzers scan the code for style violations, potential bugs, and security issues.

5. Unit tests

Automated tests that verify the functionality of individual code units are executed.

6. Integration tests

Relatively fast tests may be run to verify the interaction between different components of the code.

7. Feedback

The pipeline provides feedback to the developer about the PR's status (success/failure) and any issues found. This feedback is displayed directly in the PR on the hosted repository.

This pipeline detects and notifies developers of any issues within their code. The build step determines whether the code changes have broken the build. The test steps answer the following questions: Does this code do what is intended? Does this code include security vulnerabilities, unsafe operations, potential bugs, bad practices, deprecated features, or even inconsistent formatting?

The code pipeline provides developers with near-real-time feedback by detecting issues and running fast tests when pull requests are opened or updated. It answers critical questions about the code's functionality, security, and quality. Developers can then quickly address problems, refine the PR, or confidently merge it when all checks pass, accelerating development and ensuring a robust codebase.

(In Chapter 4, we'll explore a complementary CI pipeline triggered when a PR is merged. This pipeline deploys new code to test environments and executes longer-running test suites.)

Note that while our sample pipeline uses a code change trigger, CI/CD systems typically offer other trigger options, like scheduled and manual triggers, for more flexibility.

The Essential Build Step

The build step involves packaging code into a deployable artifact. Examples of deployable artifacts include container images (used to deploy in Kubernetes/serverless environments), language-specific packages (such as JAR, npm, NuGet, etc.), and mobile application packages (such as APK or IPA), among others. For example, code written in a compiled language, like C++, is first compiled and then linked to create machine code. Interpreted languages often require a build step to package code into an intermediate format, such as a Java Archive (JAR) file, for compilation at runtime. Other interpreted languages, including JavaScript, can be transpiled or minified to optimize for execution.

Depending on the type of code, this step or series of steps relies on build automation tools, task runners, or build scripts.

Build automation tools orchestrate the entire build process. Popular examples of automation tools include the following:

Make and CMake
> Make is one of the oldest and most fundamental build tools. It uses a Makefile to define dependencies between files and the commands needed to build them. CMake is a newer cross-platform build system generator that can generate Makefiles, Visual Studio projects, and other build scripts. It's widely used for C and C++ projects.

Ant

An early Java-based build tool that uses XML to describe the build process. It's known for its flexibility and cross-platform compatibility.

Maven

Another popular Java build tool that goes beyond just compilation. It manages dependencies, builds, tests, and packages projects.

Gradle

A newer build tool that combines the best of Ant and Maven. It uses a Groovy-based DSL to define builds and offers a more flexible and concise syntax.

Bazel

Developed by Google, Bazel is a powerful build system designed for large-scale projects. It's known for its speed, scalability, and support for multiple languages.

MSBuild

A build automation platform commonly used with .NET frameworks and languages like C#, Visual Basic .NET, and F#.

Cargo

Cargo is a package manager for the Rust programming language, used to build, compile, and manage Rust projects.

Task runners automate repetitive tasks in the development workflow, such as minification, concatenation, and transpilation. Widely used task runners for JavaScript include the following:

npm scripts

Part of the Node Package Manager (npm), npm scripts are simple scripts defined in the *package.json* file that can automate common tasks like starting a development server, running tests, and building for production.

Gulp

A streaming build system that uses JavaScript code to define tasks. It's known for its speed and efficiency in processing files.

Grunt

Another task runner for JavaScript projects, Grunt uses configuration files to define tasks. It's known for its vast ecosystem of plug-ins.

Webpack

A module bundler primarily used for JavaScript applications. It can bundle JavaScript, CSS, and other assets into optimized files for production.

Rollup
> Another module bundler that's known for its focus on generating smaller and more efficient bundles than Webpack.

Lastly, build scripts are custom scripts (often written in Bash, Python, or other scripting languages) that define the specific steps and commands needed to build a project. These can be used in conjunction with build automation tools or task runners.

Prioritizing Quality and Security with Static Analysis

Immediately after we build our code, we run static analysis tools, which may include a linter. Linters are a specific type of static analysis tool used to check coding style (ensuring, for example, consistent formatting and naming patterns); for interpreted languages like JavaScript, linters check for typos, missing semicolons, or incorrect language usage. These tools examine source code without executing it, similar to proofreading a document before publishing it. They help identify potential issues early in the development process. Static code analysis encompasses a range of techniques to evaluate code for:

Potential bugs
> Identifies common programming errors, like null pointer dereferences, resource leaks, or logic flaws

Security vulnerabilities
> Detects insecure coding practices that could lead to SQL injections, cross-site scripting (XSS), or other exploits

Code smells
> Flags maintainability issues, like duplicate code, excessive complexity, or unused variables, suggesting areas for refactoring

Adherence to standards
> Enforces coding guidelines and, sometimes, best practices specific to a language or project, ensuring consistency and readability

By integrating these static analysis tools into the early stages of the development process, we not only ensure code quality but also implement a best practice referred to as shift-left security. Shift-left security refers to the strategy of implementing security practices in the earliest stages of development. We'll dig into shift-left security and also explore how AI can help remediate security issues quickly in Chapter 5.

Automated Testing: Test Early, Test Often

Automated testing is fundamental to the CI/CD pipeline. After our example pipeline runs static analysis checks, it executes unit and integration tests against new code. Let's look at these test types:

Unit tests

> These tests validate the smallest isolated pieces of code (units), such as functions or methods, to verify that they behave as expected in isolation. Imagine a simple weather application that fetches weather data from an external API, processes it, and displays it to the user. Unit tests might test functions that process raw weather data, validating that they correctly convert the data into the desired formats. The tests validate the conversion logic alone.

Integration tests

> These tests focus on verifying the interactions between software modules, ensuring proper communication and data exchange. Integration tests are relatively fast, often conducted after unit testing, and, like unit tests, help identify issues early. An integration test for the same weather app might focus on how the data fetching and processing modules interact. These tests could verify that the app correctly retrieves and handles weather data from the API, including error scenarios, using partial mocking to simulate real-world API responses. Unlike unit tests, which isolate components, integration tests assess how multiple components work together. Integration tests that are used early in the pipeline, such as in our example pipeline, should avoid slow operations such as accessing a database, file system, or other external systems.

Unit and integration test frameworks are numerous and vary by language, for example:

Java

> JUnit 5 and TestNG are frameworks for unit testing. Mockito and Spring are used for Java integration testing.

JavaScript

> Jest and Mocha for JavaScript are widely used for unit testing. Jest also supports integration testing.

Python

> pyTest and pyUnit (UnitTest) are options for both unit and integration testing.

.NET

> NUnit and xUnit for .NET are options for unit testing, whereas Moq and NSubstitute are commonly used for integration testing.

Ruby

RSpec supports both unit and integration testing for Ruby.

Mobile (iOS/Android)

XCTest for iOS and Espresso for Android are standard bearers for mobile unit and integration testing.

Unit and integration tests act as a first line of defense, alerting developers to potential bugs or regressions in their code. These quick, automated checks are just the beginning of our testing strategy. In Chapter 4, we'll look at a subsequent pipeline that is triggered when the PR is closed and merged.

Thoroughly testing each unit of code, including all possible scenarios, results in a large but crucial suite of tests—even for seemingly simple code. However, since unit tests are isolated and don't rely on external resources, they execute rapidly.

Our pipeline prioritizes these speedy unit tests as the foundation, followed by integration tests that verify how different components work together, and finally, a smaller number of comprehensive end-to-end tests that simulate real-world usage.

In "The Test Pyramid", we'll look at the Test Pyramid framework, which illustrates how to balance different test types for optimal software quality.

The Test Pyramid

The Test Pyramid provides a model for structuring our tests strategically, prioritizing different types based on their scope and speed. While the Test Pyramid is sometimes depicted with specific test types at each layer, we prefer to conceptualize layers that encompass broad classes of tests, as shown in Figure 3-3.

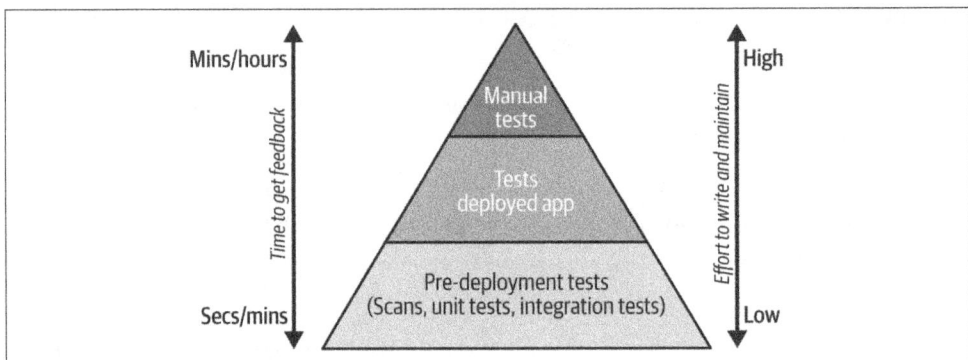

Figure 3-3. Large sets of fast tests make up the base of the Test Pyramid; smaller sets of slower tests form the higher layers

At the base of our pyramid are pre-deployment tests, which include types like unit tests, integration tests, and static scans. These tests are small and execute quickly.

Integration testing can refer to a range of test strategies. Integration tests that don't interact with external systems like databases and network services are fast and are included at this level. The wide pyramid base reflects that the suite of these types of tests should be large and, ideally, cover the complete codebase. Tests should be designed to provide fast feedback to the developer.

Moving up the pyramid, we depict the middle layer as including any type of tests that we execute against deployed code in a pre-production, test environment. Generally, these tests are typically slower than the ones mentioned above but provide valuable insights into how the system functions as a whole.

At the peak of the pyramid, we find manual tests. These are slow and labor-intensive and occur after the code has been vetted by layers of automated testing.

Embracing the pyramid approach allows teams to balance speed, cost, and effectiveness in their testing efforts. By focusing on a solid foundation of small and fast tests and supplementing them with strategic testing against deployed code, we can achieve comprehensive test coverage while minimizing the time and resources required.

A robust testing strategy is key to a streamlined pipeline, accelerating the delivery of high-quality releases. In "Continuous Integration Tools" we'll consider how the CI tool choice can prioritize that factor.

Continuous Integration Tools

Effective CI processes are essential for modern development teams. In this section, we'll look at legacy CI tools and the features that characterize modern tools.

A major national retailer—a client of ours—anticipating a surge in digital demand found itself at a crossroads. Its legacy CI/CD tools, including Jenkins, were fragmented across client web, mobile, and backend service teams, causing long build times that cost the company a staggering $500,000 annually in idle developer time. These tools not only stifled innovation but also posed significant security risks, further exacerbated by the $800,000 spent yearly on maintenance and custom scripts. This substantial investment diverted resources away from enhancing the customer experience. Faced with mounting challenges and escalating costs, the retailer sought a unified CI/CD platform to streamline operations, accelerate innovation, and fortify security.

The company's compounding challenges shed light on the inherent limitations of Jenkins, especially as organizations scale and digital demands intensify. Let's look at some of those limitations.

Jenkins Considered

Jenkins deserves credit for bringing continuous integration into the mainstream. An open source automation server, Jenkins leverages a vast ecosystem of plug-ins that extend its functionality and features and give users the ability to customize their pipelines endlessly. The Jenkins plug-in marketplace is a central repository where users can find and install thousands of these community-developed plug-ins. The Jenkins community is large and its documentation is extensive. It is an adaptable solution for diverse development environments.

While Jenkins remains valuable for legacy systems due to its specialized plug-ins (e.g., mainframes), modern CI pipelines demand more. Today's development environments require CI tools that deliver speed, security, collaborative workflows, and native integration with cloud technologies across multiple providers, Kubernetes orchestration, and containerized applications. The following sections explore specific challenges that make Jenkins less suitable for these modern requirements.

Plug-in complexity

The flexibility and extensive plug-in ecosystem of Jenkins often leads to a complex and fragmented architecture, hindering maintainability and increasing developer toil. The reliance on Groovy scripts for pipeline customization can make troubleshooting and updates cumbersome, especially as the number of pipelines and their complexity grows.

In addition, modern CI/CD solutions often embrace the "pipeline-as-code" paradigm, using declarative languages like YAML to define pipelines. This approach is generally considered more straightforward and maintainable than the scripting-heavy approach of Jenkins. YAML-based pipelines are generally more human-readable and easier to maintain (there might be exceptions) than Groovy scripts, which can become complex and harder to debug as pipelines grow in size and complexity. Defining pipelines as code allows them to be stored in VCSs alongside the application code. This ensures that pipeline changes are tracked, reviewed, and auditable, enabling better collaboration among team members. Thus, the pipeline-as-code approach allows for better version control, collaboration, and easier troubleshooting.

Lastly, the need to manage a multitude of plug-ins, each with its own configuration, introduces maintenance overhead. Team members find themselves spending valuable time on mundane tasks like resolving plug-in conflicts, updating dependencies, and deciphering cryptic error messages. This detracts from the focus on innovation and core development, slowing down innovation and delivering features.

Scalability challenges

The architecture of Jenkins, primarily designed for single-server setups, often struggles to scale efficiently as the number of jobs, pipelines, and users increases. This can lead to performance bottlenecks, slower build times, and overall system instability. While Jenkins offers distributed builds and clustering options, setting up and maintaining these solutions can be complex and resource-intensive, requiring specialized expertise and significant overhead. As a result, scaling Jenkins horizontally (*https://oreil.ly/6qFLO*) to meet the demands of large organizations or high-throughput CI/CD workflows often becomes a major challenge.

Security concerns

While Jenkins plug-ins provide extensibility, they also introduce potential vulnerabilities. Each plug-in, with its own codebase and dependencies, expands the attack surface of a Jenkins instance. Monitoring these plug-ins for vulnerabilities and ensuring timely updates becomes ongoing overhead for administrators. Furthermore, configuring Jenkins security, including user permissions, access controls, and network configurations, can be intricate. Misconfigurations can expose the system to unauthorized access or malicious activities. The dynamic nature of the plug-in ecosystem and the potential for misconfigurations mean you must be vigilant in monitoring risks and proactive in mitigating risks within your Jenkins environment.

Resource usage and efficiency concerns

Jenkins's resource consumption can be a significant drawback, especially as the number of jobs and plug-ins increases. The Java-based architecture (JVM's runtime requirements, garbage collection behavior, and framework abstractions) often leads to high memory usage, and managing numerous concurrent builds can put a strain on CPU and disk resources. This can result in slower build times, increased infrastructure costs, and potential performance issues. In larger environments, scaling Jenkins horizontally can become complex and resource-intensive, requiring additional hardware and careful configuration.

In addition, building Docker images in CI pipelines can quickly become resource-intensive and expensive, particularly when dealing with large codebases or frequent commits that trigger numerous parallel builds. Each image requires computational resources, storage space, and network bandwidth—costs that multiply across environments and branches. Similarly, while comprehensive observability provides valuable system insights, implementing excessive logging can create its own problems: storage costs surge, signal-to-noise ratios decrease, and processing overhead increases. Finding the right balance between comprehensive coverage and resource efficiency remains a critical challenge.

Beyond Jenkins

Due to the limitations of Jenkins, companies like our national retailer often outgrow it and seek modern, fully managed solutions that offer:

Built-in, fully supported building blocks
> Modern CI/CD tools offer extensive libraries of built-in, fully supported building blocks that streamline pipeline setup. This eliminates reliance on community-maintained plug-ins, ensuring reliability and stability. However, recognizing the need for customization, most solutions still support extensibility through custom plug-ins. This empowers teams to automate unique workflows and tailor the CI/CD environment to their specific needs.

Pipelines define declaratively
> Modern CI/CD tools streamline pipeline definition using declarative code like YAML, making them more accessible and easier to maintain than the Groovy scripts for Jenkins. This accelerates setup and minimizes errors associated with manual scripting.

Native support for containerization and orchestration
> Jenkins predates the widespread adoption of Docker and Kubernetes, and while Jenkins pipelines can use plug-ins to work with and orchestrate containers, the lack of native support often results in cumbersome configurations. Newer tools, in contrast, seamlessly incorporate containerization and orchestration features, simplifying the deployment and management of applications in containerized environments.

In the next sections, we'll look at additional modern features that tools newer than Jenkins offer. Before we turn our attention to these features, let's consider a fundamental question when considering CI/CD tools: whether to host and manage tools yourself or select a fully managed solution. The decision will impact everything from development velocity and cost-effectiveness to maintenance requirements. Given the importance of mobile, it's essential to select a CI/CD setup that handles the complexities of building and deploying mobile applications and we'll look at the factors specific to mobile app development to consider.

Hosting options

Organizations have three primary build infrastructure choices for their CI/CD systems: self-hosted on-premises, self-hosted cloud, and vendor-hosted (cloud). Each option presents unique benefits and drawbacks that should be carefully considered:

Self-hosted, on-prem solutions
> Self-hosting a CI/CD system on-premises gives you complete control and ownership over its infrastructure and data. This approach allows for maximum customization, enabling tailoring to specific security protocols and organizational

needs. Additionally, some organizations may prefer the one-time payment model associated with on-prem solutions. However, this approach comes with several drawbacks. It necessitates substantial up-front investment in hardware and software, as well as time and effort to maintain and update. The demand for ongoing maintenance and potential scalability challenges can strain resources, particularly for smaller organizations.

Self-hosted, cloud solutions

The self-managed, cloud-hosted model strikes a balance between control and scalability. Organizations maintain control over their CI/CD software while leveraging the cloud's flexibility and scalability. This approach reduces the need for physical hardware and simplifies scaling compared to on-prem solutions.

Cloud-hosted applications run within virtualized environments called hypervisors, and when considering cloud hosting, the type of hypervisor you select will impact simplicity and performance. The two types of hypervisors to understand are:

Type 1 bare-metal hypervisor

These run directly on the hardware, offering superior performance and isolation but requiring dedicated hardware.

Type 2, embedded hypervisors

These run on top of an operating system, providing easier setup and flexibility but potentially with lower performance.

Bare metal might be better for demanding, high-security setups, while embedded could be suitable for less intensive needs and budget constraints.

Any cloud-hosted toolset will require ongoing maintenance and updates, and your organization will remain responsible for managing the cloud infrastructure. This can lead to challenges similar to those of on-prem solutions, albeit with potentially reduced up-front costs.

Fully managed, vendor-hosted solutions

Vendor-hosted CI/CD solutions offer a fully managed service where the vendor handles infrastructure, maintenance, and updates. Your organization focuses on development rather than infrastructure management. These solutions are highly scalable, easy to use, and often follow a pay-as-you-go model, making them cost-effective. However, they may offer less customization than self-hosted options and potentially limit your organization's ability to tailor the system to your specific needs. Additionally, concerns about data security and potential vendor lock-in can arise with this approach.

Mobile app development–specific challenges

Having a robust and efficient CI/CD solution is crucial to keep pace with the fast release cycles and high-quality apps that mobile users expect. Developing for mobile brings unique challenges: your processes and your CI/CD tools must be able to manage device fragmentation and frequent mobile OS updates.

When choosing between self-hosted and fully managed CI/CD solutions, consider that self-hosted solutions, while offering control and customization, can lead to challenges like physical hardware constraints. In addition, your team will be responsible for constant maintenance and updates to build environments. These complexities can lead to unexpected costs. The frequent release cycles of tools like Xcode for iOS development necessitate regular hardware updates, which can be a significant time and resource drain for any team.

Fully managed CI/CD solutions, on the other hand, alleviate these pain points by providing automatic updates to build environments and predictable costs. This allows your team to focus on building features and improving their apps rather than managing infrastructure. Moreover, fully managed CI/CD solutions specifically optimized for mobile development offer mobile-specific integrations and features that streamline the development process. Many of these platforms fully manage challenges of mobile development, such as device fragmentation and OS updates, for you.

Modern Features to Accelerate Software Builds

Returning to our retailer: it researched newer options and decided to move on from Jenkins and the set of plug-ins and tools pieced together to work with it. The company selected a unified platform that simplified its toolset while providing the scalability and cost savings that it required. It was able to consolidate CI/CD processes for services, client web, and mobile teams onto this single platform. The new platform eliminated the need for extensive scripting, saving developers time and enabling them to focus on innovation. It also leveraged AI/ML for testing, resulting in further cost savings and much faster builds. Furthermore, a unified platform improved security by supporting security testing early in the pipeline, enabling faster detection and remediation of vulnerabilities. The efficiency, security, and reliability of the new platform enabled the retailer to easily handle its digital growth.

In the next sections, we will look at features in modern systems that enable faster, cost-effective, and secure pipelines.

Accelerate builds with caching

Modern build environments are ephemeral, enhancing agility by providing isolated, cost-effective, and scalable setups that accelerate development cycles while maintaining consistency across stages of the CI/CD pipeline. However, ephemeral environments require setting up the entire build process from scratch each time, including

---

downloading dependencies, compiling code, and generating artifacts. This is time-consuming.

Caching is a technique used in CI/CD to store and reuse build artifacts, dependencies, Docker layers, and intermediate results. This significantly reduces build times by avoiding redundant operations and focusing on building only what has changed, which not only speeds up development cycles but also conserves computational resources and energy. Modern CI/CD systems intelligently manage this caching process, optimizing builds without manual intervention. Caching can be done at different stages—caching software dependencies, caching Docker layers, and caching build outputs from tools like Bazel, Gradle, and Maven.

Streamline building, caching, and testing with AI

An AI-native CI solution will seamlessly integrate GenAI, agentic AI, and MCP to enhance building the software, caching required components, and testing each build. Let's look at these enhancements in more detail.

Build phase enhancements. GenAI can automate boilerplate code creation for repetitive tasks (e.g., Dockerfile templates, CI configuration files), reducing manual effort. It can also analyze historical build data to predict dependency conflicts and suggest optimal versions, minimizing build failures. Another interesting use case for GenAI is generating optimized CI pipeline YAML configurations based on project structure, reducing trial-and-error setups.

Agentic AI can detect build failures (e.g., missing dependencies), and can then automatically retry with corrected configurations and log root causes. It can also dynamically scale build resources (e.g., cloud instances) based on workload demands, balancing speed and cost, and can dynamically split monolithic builds into parallelizable tasks, reducing execution time.

MCP can standardize environment variables, build flags, and toolchain versions across distributed teams, ensuring consistency and sharing prebuilt artifacts, such as compiled libraries, between related projects via MCP's centralized cache, avoiding redundant builds.

Cache phase enhancements. GenAI can be used to make the caching techniques more intelligent. It can predict which dependencies (e.g., *node_modules*, *.m2* artifacts) will be needed based on code changes, precaching them before builds start. ML models can be used to identify stale caches by analyzing code diff patterns, ensuring only relevant artifacts are retained. Agentic AI can flag and purge poisoned caches (e.g., corrupted artifacts) in real time, preventing failed builds.

Using MCP in scalable infrastructure has many advantages, including enabling secure, low-latency cache sharing across CI pipelines via standardized APIs, and reducing redundant data transfers by caching intermediate build outputs (e.g., Docker layers) between CI runs. MCP can enable secure cache sharing between parallel CI jobs through standardized APIs, eliminating redundant builds in monorepo architectures.

Test phase enhancements.   Consider a scenario where a developer modifies a single line of code in a seldom-used component within a large application. We have high code coverage with our large and robust set of unit tests; these are the foundation of our test strategy, the base of our Test Pyramid. Yet, when little code has changed, executing the entire test suite results in lengthy, resource-intensive, and very inefficient test cycles.

Modern tools can mitigate these issues with AI tooling that intelligently selects and executes only the tests directly relevant to the modified code. This approach significantly reduces the time and resources required for testing, leading to faster feedback loops and more efficient development processes.

Harness Test Intelligence (TI) (*https://oreil.ly/_-jPi*) is an example of this approach. Let's look at how TI works under the hood. Three components work together to enable Harness TI:

TI service
> This service uses AI and understands your repository, Git commits, and unit tests and uses this data to dynamically build a graph that maps the relationships between code methods and their corresponding unit tests. This graph is continuously updated to reflect changes in the codebase.

A test runner agent
> This component communicates with the service and executes tests.

A test step
> This is the step you add to your CI pipeline to integrate TI into your workflow.

The TI workflow begins when a developer initiates a pull request and triggers the pipeline. The TI service analyzes the code changes and compares them to its graph to identify the tests that need to be executed. It considers not only the code modifications but also any changes or additions to the tests themselves. This ensures that all relevant aspects of the codebase are thoroughly tested while avoiding redundant test runs.

Thus, by focusing on the impacted tests, intelligent testing approaches can significantly reduce the testing time, especially in large projects with extensive test suites. This translates to faster builds and faster feedback for developers, allowing them to identify and address issues more quickly.

AI-powered build and test insights

Modern CI/CD tools also leverage GenAI to automate tedious tasks and provide insights when things go wrong. For example, a tool can autogenerate your pipelines, analyze code for potential issues, and troubleshoot build and deployment failures in real time. If a CI build fails, GenAI can analyze log files, pinpoint the error, and even suggest potential fixes. This saves your time, reduces downtime, and accelerates the software delivery process.

Agentic AI can also be used to come up with recommendations to optimize existing pipelines based on your organization's golden standards. This feature would be extremely valuable since organizations, more often than not, optimize their current pipelines rather than create new pipelines.

Another excellent use case for GenAI is writing intent-based tests. Testing, especially UI testing, can be extremely manual and flaky if the UI changes. By using GenAI, developers and QA engineers can simply state the intent of a test and let GenAI figure out the steps. We will discuss intent-based testing in detail in Chapter 4.

Finally, AI can also be used to generate data for tests ethically and responsibly. Some examples include ensuring compliance with GDPR and other regulations when using production data for model training, maintaining data privacy and security throughout the data generation process, and using proper algorithms to generate synthetic data.

Unify CI/CD metrics with enterprise observability

A modern CI/CD solution should be a team player, working with the other key platforms in your corporate ecosystem, particularly the observability platform that your organization relies on to understand system behavior, identify performance bottlenecks, and proactively detect and resolve issues before they impact users or business operations. Observability platforms include Elastic with Logstash and Kibana, a popular open source platform, and Datadog and Splunk, well-known commercial options.

Modern continuous integration tools provide telemetry data to these platforms by implementing OpenTelemetry, an open source framework. This brings in CI/CD metrics to enable observability and dashboards that can help you understand what's happening and improve build performance and reliability.

Modern CI/CD support for monorepos

Versioning and dependency management become very challenging when managing complex codebases across several repositories. Monorepos are single repositories that contain all the code for a project or organization, providing a centralized approach to managing complex codebases. A single repository simplifies dependency management by keeping a single copy of any shared library or component, and simplifies code sharing and reuse across different projects. While monorepos increase the risk of merge conflicts and require careful design to avoid tightly coupled code, many large companies have successfully adopted them for massive codebases, demonstrating that an effectively managed monorepo can provide a very scalable approach.

When adopting a monorepo strategy, it's important to understand the unique requirements that monorepos make of code repositories and CI tools. With potentially hundreds of developers contributing to a large monorepo, managing changes and pull requests efficiently becomes critical. Teams must be able to define appropriate access by subdirectories, in part to ensure that only relevant reviewers are notified for each change. Repositories should support subdirectory-specific ownership.

Monorepos require CI systems that enable selective building and testing of changed components and that support advanced dependency management, caching, and parallel execution. Tools like Harness CI support these needs through features like path-based triggers, which run pipelines only when specific directories in the repository change (e.g., triggering service A's pipeline for changes to *serviceA/*), and sparse checkout, which clones a subdirectory instead of the entire repository. This optimizes resource usage and speeds up feedback loops while maintaining dependency integrity.

Summary

CI has become an indispensable practice, reducing integration issues, providing faster feedback, and improving overall efficiency. In this chapter, we looked at modern, fully managed CI/CD tool features, contrasting the trade-offs with the costs and challenges of self-hosting. We looked at the importance of prioritizing faster, smaller unit tests for quick feedback, followed by slower test types for comprehensive coverage. The continuous integration pipeline we looked at exemplified this practice: in the context of opening a PR, we build, complete static scans, and then run quick tests to ensure our code does what it should and doesn't introduce regressions. We also explored various ways in which an AI-native CI tool could use GenAI, agentic AI, and MCP to enhance the build, cache, and test phases of CI.

In Chapter 4, we'll continue with CI/CD and focus on deploying to test environments and executing the slower tests that evaluate the system's performance, resiliency, and end-to-end behavior.

Deploying to Test Environments

In Chapter 3, we explored the fundamentals of continuous integration, focusing on early steps in a CI/CD pipeline: mainly, building and pre-deployment testing. We walked through an example pipeline triggered when a PR is opened, as shown in Figure 4-1.

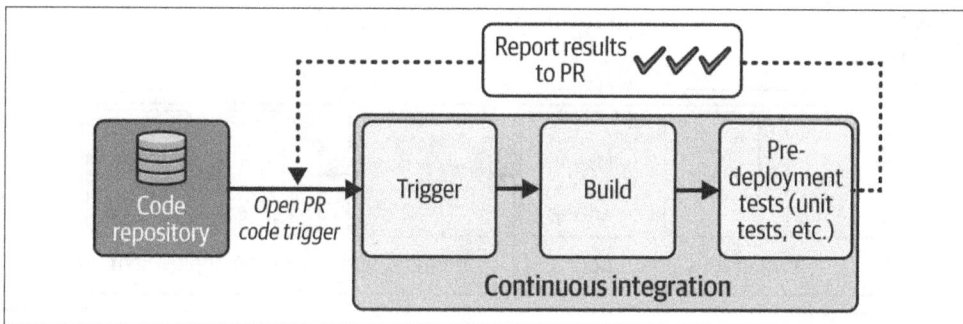

Figure 4-1. A CI pipeline

This pipeline built and packaged the code, conducted static code analysis, and executed early, fast tests including unit and lightweight integration tests, providing build and test feedback to the PR. These steps ensure that the code in the pull request is merge-ready, providing confidence that the merged code would function as intended and would not introduce any regressions. Assuming that the code changes in the PR prove ready, the developer can merge the PR.

With our new code merged, the next step is getting ready for production by deploying into test environments and then running a battery of tests. AI and ML tools are being integrated into the deployment process. These tools help teams make better deployment decisions, identify potential issues proactively, and streamline the verification process. Rather than adding complexity, well-implemented AI actually reduces the cognitive load on developers while improving deployment reliability.

Between the CI steps and the production release, we are primarily focused on testing. We want to learn if the release is ready for our users. If it is safe to release, we want to get it to our users quickly, to enhance the user experience and potentially drive increased customer engagement and loyalty. If our software has a problem, we need to detect and address it quickly. That dynamic is a barrier to releasing valuable updates, and the longer the time between the introduction of the defect and when it is brought back to the development team, the less likely the work will be fresh in the mind of the developers involved. They will have to spend more time and effort familiarizing themselves with those sections of code, making the remediation more expensive. If a developer is already deep into their next task, that task may be interrupted and become more expensive to complete as well.

When the release is ready, we will deploy the release into one or more environments where we can test against running code. It is in these pre-production environments that we bridge the gap between development and real-world usage, ensuring our software not only functions correctly but is ready for real-world scenarios.

Figure 4-2 gives a high-level depiction of our entire delivery process. Increasingly, AI is being embedded throughout this pipeline to strengthen testing and deployment decisions.

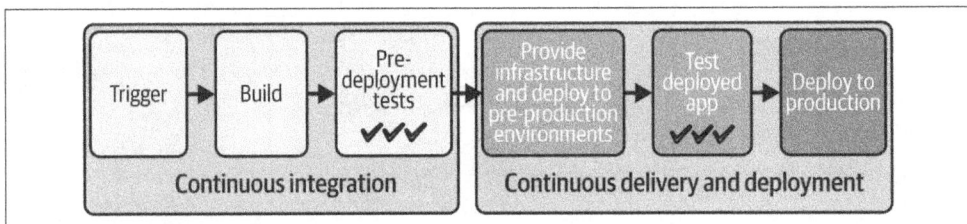

Figure 4-2. High-level delivery process

In this chapter we'll look at steps to provision infrastructure, deploy to one or more pre-production environments, and test against the software. In addition, we will cover key best practices including:

- Using IaC to create the lower environments that are consistent with production, but smaller
- Using "production-like" deployments to move your application consistently
- Connecting testing to the deployment pipeline
- Selecting where to apply AI to deployments and where to remain cautious

This stage in the pipeline is a pivotal one, where development and operations concerns intersect. By understanding and implementing these best practices, you'll be well-equipped to determine the optimal number and types of test environments for your specific project requirements, regardless of project size or complexity. You will understand how to balance development velocity and operational stability, ensuring your software undergoes thorough testing and is release-ready.

Establishing a Unified Deployment Process

As we continue to navigate our delivery pipeline en route to production, we need to consider the deployment steps and deployment environments that will be necessary. For a delivery process that is predictable and reliable, we need deployment steps and environments that are predictable and reliable.

In this section, we'll cover best practices to give us the predictability and reliability we're after, from test to production. In Chapter 8 we will cover production releases and production environments in greater detail.

Deploy Consistently to Every Environment

Automation is the foundation of DevOps, and a key function of our delivery pipeline is to automate both the setup of our pre-production environments and the deployments to those environments. Just as we need to validate our software before releasing it into the wild, we need to have measures in place to validate how we deploy our software.

We do this by consistently using the same methods to deploy to pre-production environments as we do to deploy to production. This consistency tests our deployment methods and minimizes the risk of unexpected issues when repeating these steps to deploy our software into production environments.

The following best practices help provide the predictability we're after.

Use consistent tooling

It's not unusual for developers to spin up their own lightweight deployment processes using simple tooling to deploy to test environments, while the operations teams focus on processes geared to production deployments using enterprise tooling. This inconsistency between processes leads to changes being communicated on an "as broken basis," where developers will update their process and forget to notify operations until something breaks.

This approach should be avoided, as it limits the effectiveness of testing in nonproduction environments and leads to duplicated effort in automation scripting. Instead, adopt a unified toolset for all deployments.

One way to encourage consistency is to offer developers easy, premade template pipelines known as "golden pipelines" or "paved roads." We will examine this in more detail in Chapter 10. At a minimum, your developers and operations teams need to agree on a common set of tools for performing deployments.

Use consistent pipeline steps and deployment strategies

Whether you're using your CI/CD tool or custom deployment scripts, the sequence of actions should remain consistent across environments. Advanced deployment strategies like canary or blue-green deployments are typically selected based on derisking production deployments. If your production environment utilizes these strategies, replicate them in your pre-production environments. Similarly, if you were to use feature flags to release individual features in production, use feature flags to roll out the features in test environments. This consistency minimizes the chance of introducing discrepancies or oversights during deployment.

We'll cover production deployment and these progressive deployment strategies more thoroughly in Chapters 7 and 8. For now, note that the steps and strategies you use should be replicated at every level. While a test environment may be smaller due to cost or resource constraints, deploy as if it were a production environment. For example, a rolling deployment in production might deploy two nodes at a time to 10 targets, while in a test environment you could deploy one node at a time to 3 targets. This approach ensures that your production deployment steps and strategy are thoroughly tested with each version deployed to the test environment.

In Chapter 7, we will examine in depth how AI techniques can verify that a deployment is not causing trouble in its new environment. Those same approaches should be used in lower environments to validate that they are working and protect our tests from being run against a faulty install.

Use parameterization for differences

Inevitably, variations will exist between environments. Target names, service URLs, and passwords may differ. Instead of creating unique deployment scripts for each environment, leverage variables to accommodate these differences. This allows you to maintain a single, adaptable script or pipeline that can be tailored to the specific environment at runtime.

By being consistent in deployment, you'll create a robust and reliable delivery pipeline that instills confidence in your team's ability to release software seamlessly and efficiently.

Accelerate pipeline creation with AI

In Chapter 3, we discussed automatic pipeline creation. Templating remains a good pattern—you want your AI to leverage your organization's templates and pull in the correct adjustments and variables for your project and team. Whether you or an AI are creating or maintaining pipelines, the less that pipeline code needs to be managed, the better.

Leverage Infrastructure as Code for deployment consistency

We want consistent and predictable environments to deliver our release to production. IaC gives us an approach to not only achieve consistency but also control our configuration with as much care and control as we do our code resources. At its core, IaC treats infrastructure configuration like software code.

Engineers make changes to the IaC code locally and test them in their development environment. These changes are then committed to the VCS, just like application code. By managing our IaC, we leverage these features of our VCS and CI/CD pipelines.

The as-code nature has made IaC a DevOps area that quickly benefited from large language models. AI coding assistants generate and explain IaC code well, lowering the barriers to entry for developers and infrastructure professionals adopting new IaC languages. For major cloud providers with access to performance data from environments or DevOps platforms that combine cloud cost features with IaC management, future code generation tools will likely incorporate the following runtime optimizations based on live workloads:

Collaboration and code review
  Version control enables multiple team members to work on files simultaneously and manage conflicts. We can define and enforce policies to require code reviews of our infrastructure configuration changes.

Branching and experimentation
  Version control allows you to create branches for experimenting with different configurations without affecting the main production environment.

Traceability and auditability
  A VCS provides a complete history of changes to your configuration settings. The commit messages and change history help you understand why your systems evolve, and audit trails are important in supporting compliance with security frameworks.

Rollback and recovery
  If an infrastructure configuration change causes problems, you can quickly revert to a previous working version, minimizing downtime and impact on your systems. In addition, in the case of a catastrophic failure, you can use your version-controlled configurations to restore your systems to a known working state.

Automated testing

Delivery pipelines can run automated tests on the IaC code, including syntax checks, security scans, and compliance tests. The changes are then applied to the staging environment for integration testing, and finally, they're promoted to production, typically using a careful rollout strategy.

Security

Version control can help enforce security policies and controls around configuration changes, ensuring that only authorized personnel can make modifications.

Consider a scenario all too familiar to many in the tech industry: an application works flawlessly in development and runs smoothly in staging, but descends into chaos when deployed to production. This discrepancy often stems from inconsistencies in infrastructure configurations across environments. With IaC configuration definitions you can ensure that every environment, from development to production, is provisioned identically.

This methodical process ensures that your infrastructure evolves in a controlled, predictable manner. It eliminates the "worked in QA" problem by removing unexpected differences between environments. By treating your infrastructure with the same respect and rigor as your application code, you gain consistency, reliability, and agility.

IaC offers several advantages beyond control and consistency. With a single command, you can spin up new environments that are exact replicas of your existing infrastructure. This not only makes your processes repeatable but also serves as accurate, living documentation. Because environments are easily created and destroyed, you can tear them down when not in use, saving resources and reducing costs, with the confidence that they can be recreated effortlessly.

To implement IaC effectively, you need the right tools, and several popular options are available. Terraform and its more open fork, OpenTofu, use a cloud-agnostic approach. If you're all in on a particular cloud provider, native tools like AWS CloudFormation or Azure Resource Manager might be more appropriate.

Leverage Git Workflows with GitOps

GitOps is a newer and increasingly popular approach to deploying software that builds on the capabilities of code repositories. With a GitOps approach, you describe the desired state of infrastructure in version-controlled configuration. This description is declarative. GitOps tools include an agent that regularly reconciles the actual environment and the desired state described in Git-controlled configurations. Instead of running a script to directly deploy software, you instigate a software deployment by updating the configuration in your code repository. This approach and GitOps tools are typically used in Kubernetes environments to orchestrate containerized applications across clusters of machines.

With this approach, you rely on your code repository to enforce security, provide governance, and implement your organization's policies, such as requiring oversight through code reviews and approvals. Your updates are traceable and auditable. You can collaborate, experiment, and roll back the configuration updates used to deploy software. Once you make an update and merge it, the GitOps reconciliation agent does the rest, picking up the updates and implementing the changes to the target environment.

The approach has gained traction because managing the intricate configurations describing complex orchestrated cloud systems is an application well suited to code repository capabilities. In addition, GitOps addresses the problem of environment drift; that is, the environment is changed operationally from the desired state. The reconciliation agent automatically detects and remediates, guarding against inconsistencies in environments.

While a GitOps approach is powerful, deploying with a GitOps approach within a CI/CD delivery pipeline is more complicated than simply pushing your app updates with a script. With GitOps, your pipeline must automate the following steps:

1. Retrieve configuration from your code repository.
2. Update the configuration to reference the latest version of your application.
3. Merge the updated configuration back to Git.

GitOps reconciliation then takes it from there.

You may also encounter complexities with applications that are geographically replicated across multiple clusters. Maintaining consistency and synchronizing across clusters can be difficult due to many GitOps reconcilers being optimized for deploying applications to a single cluster. You may need to balance the need for a single source of truth with the reality that certain configurations will need to be tailored for specific clusters. Commercial GitOps tools often provide orchestration and visibility in these more complicated scenarios, extending what open source provides.

Despite these challenges, the benefits in terms of collaboration, traceability, and automated reconciliation make GitOps a compelling choice for organizations that extensively leverage Kubernetes.

Continuous Delivery, Deployment, and Test in the CI/CD Pipeline

Now that we have an understanding of the importance of predictable and reliable deployment steps and environments, let's return to our delivery pipeline. With our new code merged, we now want to deploy it into one or more environments where we can test against running code. Figure 4-3 shows an example pipeline.

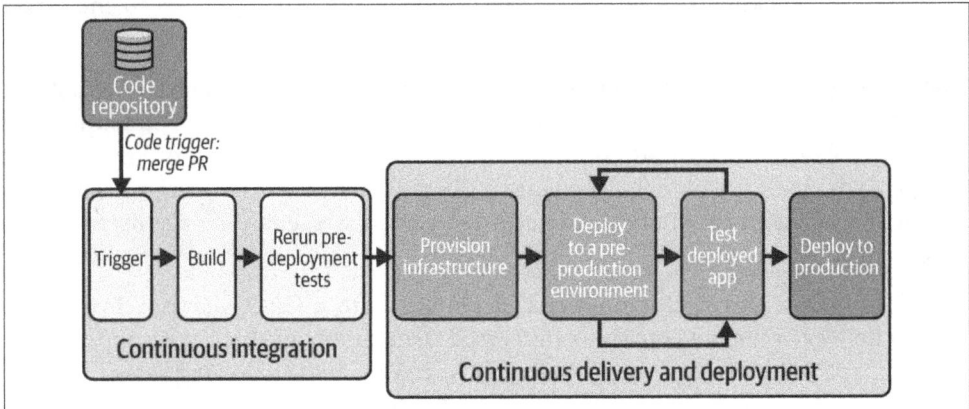

Figure 4-3. Testing our code in pre-production environments

In this section, we'll focus on the pipeline:

1. *Code trigger*

   The pull request is reviewed, approved, and merged into the main branch. In this pipeline, the PR merge triggers the pipeline.

2. *Continuous integration*

   The pipeline repeats the continuous integration steps we reviewed in the last chapter, checking out, building, and executing continuous integration tests.

3. *Provision infrastructure*

   The pipeline provisions the pre-production environments required for testing.

4. *Deploy to one or more pre-production environments*

   The pipeline deploys the app to one or more pre-production environments.

5. *Tests against the deployed app*

   The pipeline tests against the deployed software. Various types of tests can be run, depending on the type of software and the priorities of your organization. We'll look at a number of different types of tests in the following section. The pipeline can be configured to run multiple types of tests in parallel or sequentially. Some tests can reuse the same pre-production environments, while others

---

may necessitate pre-production environments tailored to the requirements of the tests. Generally, faster tests are prioritized over slower tests.

6. Deploy to production

The last step is to deploy, or promote, to the production environment. Depending on your delivery process, the decision to deploy to production can be automated or require manual approval. We'll look at promotion strategies and steps to deploy to production in Chapter 7.

Continuous Delivery Versus Continuous Deployment

The terms continuous delivery and continuous deployment are often used interchangeably. Continuous delivery is generally and loosely defined as a process that automates the software release up to the point of production deployment, requiring a manual approval before changes go live. Continuous deployment, on the other hand, fully automates the entire process, including deployment to production.

The confusion arises because pipelines automate deployments to intermediate test environments. Some use "continuous delivery" to encompass these automated intermediate deployments, while others reserve it for processes that don't deploy automatically to *any* environment. Similarly, "continuous deployment" is sometimes used broadly to describe any automated deployment, including to test environments.

To avoid confusion, we prefer to use "continuous delivery" broadly, to refer to the process of frequent delivery of software to its users. Reducing the number of manual steps will tend to make this process more frequent. When we discuss deployment steps in a specific delivery process, we include details about the deployment environments (intermediate or production) and type (automated or manual).

Types of Testing

Test environments are crucial for running tests, but the choice of tests depends heavily on the type of application being developed, the intended users, software architecture, and budget and time constraints. For example, in general, testing priorities for a website will differ significantly from those of embedded software or a web API. Testing priorities will vary between software services in a highly regulated industry versus software that must be intuitive and compelling to a large retail user base. Your selection of tests and their frequency can substantially impact application quality, infrastructure costs, and overall delivery speed.

AI-powered testing platforms increasingly use ML to optimize testing strategies. These platforms analyze historical test data, code changes, application architecture, and past deployment issues to intelligently select and prioritize tests. For example, AI-driven test selection tools identify the most impactful tests to execute for each code change, significantly speeding up test cycles. Vendors such as Harness, Tricentis SeaLights, and CloudBees Launchable are using AI and ML techniques to optimize test selection.

Here are common types of tests that occur during this phase:

End-to-end or functional tests
These tests are the most straightforward test type, simulating real-world user scenarios and validating the entire application flow from start to finish, to determine if the software does what is expected. These tests may be automated or performed manually. Modern teams automate more. Selenium is a commonly used open source test automation framework that many commercial tools also build upon. ML has been present in these tools for quite some time, but we are increasingly seeing a shift toward an AI-first approach, which we'll dive into shortly.

AI-powered testing
AI can automatically generate test cases, identify edge cases, and learn from previous test runs to focus on areas most likely to have issues. AI testing is likely to complement or be a part of your end-to-end (functional) test programs.

API tests
A form of functional testing is API testing, which validates that an API works as expected. In distributed systems, services interact over APIs, so ensuring that APIs are performing well is important. Common API testing frameworks include SoapUI, Postman, Insomnia, and Swagger. AI-enhanced API testing goes beyond simple validation to intelligently explore API behaviors and edge cases. These systems can automatically generate API test scenarios by analyzing API documentation or actual usage patterns.

User experience tests
Developers, testers, and product managers may evaluate new features to make sure they are easy and intuitive to use. While this may test the same systems as end-to-end testing, the focus is on assessing usability.

User acceptance tests
These tests are typically done as a final check to ensure that the software meets the end user's needs, that it meets the requirements, and that it functions as expected. User acceptance tests can include many other types of tests, from end-to-end to user experience and performance. These tests are done from the end user's perspective with the purpose of providing a final and formal acceptance of the software release.

Accessibility tests

These tests ensure that our software is usable for people with disabilities such as visual, hearing, or cognitive impairments in order to serve our users and comply with legal, contractual, and regulatory requirements. Open source accessibility scanners include Lighthouse and Pa11Y. Companies, including accessiBe, are beginning to offer AI-augmented testing and remediation tooling as well.

Localization tests

Localization testing is important for software targeting a global audience. It involves a comprehensive assessment of the product's linguistic accuracy, cultural appropriateness, and functional correctness within the specific target locale. This includes verifying translations, adapting visuals to cultural sensitivities, and ensuring the software functions correctly with local formats and regulations.

Performance tests

These tests simulate workloads to assess the speed, responsiveness, and stability of the application under different conditions. The tests help identify performance bottlenecks and ensure the application can handle expected traffic. This type of testing is critical for applications with seasonal peaks to ensure that the release can withstand peak demand. Apache JMeter, Gatling, and Grafana k6 are often used for performance testing. AI can leverage the data from performance testing to recommend resilience tests to run. These AI-powered performance testing systems can now detect performance anomalies with much greater accuracy than traditional threshold-based approaches. The systems establish baseline performance patterns and identify subtle deviations that might indicate looming issues. More advanced platforms can even pinpoint the specific components or code changes responsible for performance degradation by correlating test results with code changes and architecture maps.

Resilience tests

In modern distributed systems, a production system has many components. The one certainty is that something is going to break somewhere. Resilience testing, also known as chaos testing, evaluates if the software can remain useful when services it relies on fail. We'll return to resilience testing in Chapter 6.

Security tests

These tests identify vulnerabilities and weaknesses in the application that could be exploited by attackers. They help ensure the security and integrity of the application. Dynamic application security testing (DAST) is a specific type of security testing that automates penetration testing, inspecting your running application for security flaws. DAST attempts to attack your applications like a malicious user would. ZAP is a commonly used free tool, while commercial offerings from Veracode and Checkmarx are popular as well. We'll return to security testing in Chapter 5.

While the test types outlined above are commonly used, it's important to note that there is no one-size-fits-all approach to software testing, and terminology can vary across organizations. The specific tests you choose and how you categorize them will depend on your unique development process, application architecture, and risk tolerance.

Intent-Based Functional and End-to-End Testing

Traditional approaches to automated functional and end-to-end testing often rely heavily on scripted tests or simplistic record-and-playback methods. While convenient initially, these tests quickly become brittle and difficult to maintain, breaking whenever minor UI changes occur. This fragility creates a high maintenance burden, slows down development, and frequently results in teams abandoning automated testing entirely or limiting its scope.

An emerging AI-first approach to testing, known as intent-based testing, aims to overcome these challenges. Instead of explicitly scripting or manually recording each test step, teams express the intent of their test scenarios, describing the outcome they expect rather than the exact sequence of actions to achieve it. AI-native testing tools then dynamically generate and execute these tests by interacting with your application, much like a human user would.

For example, instead of recording precise clicks and form inputs for an e-commerce checkout process, you could simply describe the goal: "Purchase a product using a credit card." The AI would automatically determine the most appropriate paths through your application, interacting with buttons, forms, and workflows intelligently.

An important benefit is improved resilience of the tests—addressing the challenge of UI-based tests being brittle. If the UI changes later, the AI adapts to the new layout or modified interactions, significantly reducing maintenance overhead. Test automation tools have tried to automatically repair tests for many years, using techniques from tracking DOM objects to implementing ML. Shifting to understand the intent behind the test, and attempting to regenerate the entire script in response to a UI overhaul, brings a new level of recoverability.

These tools may also help compensate for the shift from professional testers toward asking developers to own these tests. The tools can recommend additional tests and assertions related to the existing tests, which may help an optimistic developer remember to check for corner cases and bad user behavior.

Advanced use cases for AI include migrating tests written in traditional tools such as Selenium and Playwright into intent-based testing tools, and generating and running not just individual tests but also entire test cases.

Traditional Testing Versus a Hollowing-Out-the-Middle Approach

In traditional software development, testing is often compartmentalized with dedicated environments for each type. This ensures, for example, that manual user experience testing is never impacted by concurrent automated performance tests. However, this isolation comes at a cost: a proliferation of test environments is expensive and can be time-consuming to manage. When a single new release must clear numerous stages, the approach becomes increasingly unsustainable in the face of accelerating release cadences and growing application complexity.

As you try to accelerate your release cadences and your application becomes more complex, it becomes increasingly unsustainable to test across many stages, with each stage requiring a new environment. Figure 4-4 illustrates this staged approach.

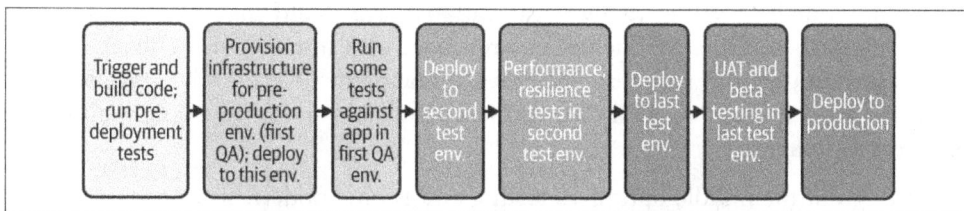

Figure 4-4. Traditional testing through several pre-production environments

On the other hand, a more modern testing approach challenges this model. This approach is sometimes referred to as "hollowing out the middle." Instead of multiple, sequential test passes across multiple environments, there are fewer environments where tests run concurrently. This practice advocates shifting testing both to the left *and to the right*.

We introduced shift-left security in Chapter 3. By moving SAST, SCA, dependency scanning, and secrets detection into pre-deployment steps, our sample pipeline exemplified shift-left. We incorporated these crucial tests early such that passing them is a prerequisite to merging code. Unit and other early testing, completed as part of the merge workflow, also represent a shift-left approach. This helps catch issues sooner, reducing the need for extensive downstream testing.

A shift-right approach advocates executing some types of tests, traditionally late-cycle test types, against the new release in the live, production environment. Instead of provisioning and moving a release from one or more pre-production environments and using these isolated environments to test, we deploy the app straight to production and validate there. For example, load testing can be difficult to execute well and the environments may need to be large. Deploying to a portion of prod, applying load to that targeted infrastructure, and measuring the impact using production observability tooling can be a viable alternative to traditional load testing. Figure 4-5 illustrates this approach.

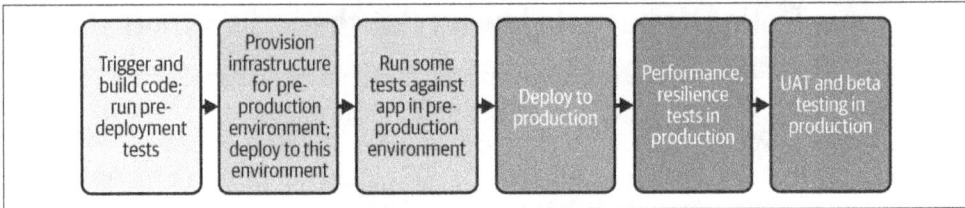

Figure 4-5. A "hollow-out-the-middle" approach to testing

We can see that removing the need for pre-production environments that closely mirror production can save costs and maintenance toil, but how can extensive testing in a production environment be safe? Shift-right relies on new tools and production deployment practices. With advanced traffic management, observability tools, and containerization, many organizations have found that these tests can in fact be performed in the production environment with minimal side effects. Beyond significantly cutting infrastructure expenses, this approach has the advantage of yielding more accurate results. We'll discuss these new tools and production deployment practices in Chapter 7.

Hollowing out the middle optimizes testing and is one modern strategy that organizations are taking to fuel faster delivery. By redesigning our approach to how we move our software between environments, we can similarly accelerate our delivery process. In "Promotion Between Environments", we'll look at how and why we should promote our releases between environments.

Promotion Between Environments

In the previous section, we looked at a typical delivery process that required moving our software through multiple stages of testing, with each stage of testing conducted in a separate pre-production environment. In this process we want to promote our release as quickly and intelligently as possible, meaning our new version of software should advance to the next environment and stage without any undue delay.

AI is beginning to play an increasing role in this promotion process, analyzing test results, performance data, and deployment history to make intelligent decisions about when and how to promote releases. These systems can evaluate multiple metrics simultaneously, detect subtle patterns that might indicate risks, and become increasingly accurate over time through ML.

Ideally, our promotion process is simple: if the tests in one stage pass, our release is immediately promoted to the next environment, and that environment is ready and available for the next round of testing. The promotion decision is automatic and instant and simply based on whether the previous stage of testing passed. In practice, release promotion, even between test environments, becomes a bottleneck in many delivery processes. This can be attributed to several factors:

Promotion decision is by committee
Promotion decisioning is not automated and requires a group review and approval of test results.

Promotion relies on tedious manual steps
Manual intervention to trigger the next deployment creates bottlenecks.

Insufficient number of testing environments
If the next environment is occupied with testing another version, the new version must wait.

In this section we'll look at mitigations to address these issues. The practices we'll introduce help us move our release from one pre-production environment to the next, and also apply to promoting our app into production. However, the final release into production has some special considerations, which will be addressed in more depth in Chapter 7.

From Decisions by Committee to Automated Decisions

Human decision making, whether it's a committee huddle or a trusted individual's call, inevitably introduces delays in promoting your release from one stage to the next. Team members need to be alerted, then take time to analyze testing results before reaching a decision and taking action. While this might not always be labor-intensive, it undoubtedly slows things down.

While traditional automation has relied on simple pass/fail criteria, AI systems offer more sophisticated decision-making capabilities. Modern AI promotion engines can evaluate hundreds of metrics simultaneously, looking beyond simple test results to analyze system behavior holistically. These systems might consider factors like performance trends, error types, user impact assessments, and even code change risk levels based on past deployment patterns. By weighting these factors appropriately, AI can make more nuanced decisions than traditional rule-based approaches.

Our aim is to streamline this process by automating the decision to promote your release. We'll revisit this topic in detail in Chapter 7.

From Manual to Automated Promotion

Once you've automated the decision-making process, the actual promotion of your build becomes significantly easier. The key is to ensure that the deployment to the next environment is triggered immediately after the decision to proceed has been made, eliminating unnecessary wait times.

How you implement this automation depends on your chosen continuous delivery tooling. Some tools offer end-to-end pipelines with simple, built-in triggers for seamless promotion between stages. Others allow you to call another pipeline or job as a step within your current pipeline, offering flexibility but potentially requiring more configuration. While the ease of implementation varies, achieving this level of automation is almost always possible.

GitOps-style deployments, however, often present a unique challenge in this area, as we discussed in "Leverage Git Workflows with GitOps." To execute the deployment, we need to automate the Git changes to the GitOps configurations instead of relying on manual updates. To do so, we will typically automate the pull request step and its approval directly within our CI/CD pipeline. We maintain Git as the source of truth that GitOps is known for while automating each step of our release promotion.

For example, imagine a scenario where your pipeline has determined that a build is ready for promotion to the User Acceptance Testing (UAT) environment. When our pipeline is set up to generate the necessary pull request, trigger any required approvals, and (once approved) merge the changes into the main branch, our pipeline initiates the GitOps deployment to the UAT environment seamlessly.

Break the Environment Bottleneck

A final challenge in automating promotion between stages and environments in your delivery process is determining the "right" number of environments that you'll need. Having too many environments becomes a financial burden due to the cost of maintaining their underlying infrastructure, while having too few creates bottlenecks and delays in moving releases toward delivery, as the process waits on resources to become available.

Ephemeral environments present a common solution to this dilemma. This approach involves creating environments on demand when needed for testing and promptly dismantling them once tests are complete. In the pre-cloud era, environment creation was a laborious process, often taking days. Now, thanks to programmable cloud infrastructure, environments can be spun up and torn down in minutes.

Infrastructure as Code Management (IaCM) tools simplify ephemeral environments. These specialized CI/CD platforms automate the provisioning, configuration, and deployment of infrastructure resources using code. Unlike traditional CI/CD tools focused on applications, IaCM tools manage the underlying infrastructure. With IaCM tools, you define your desired infrastructure state using declarative code templates, making configurations more manageable, maintainable, and version-controlled.

Ideally, to achieve our goal of "production-like" test environments, the same template should be used to create both pre-production test environments and production environments, with adjustments made only to variables. When your pipelines seamlessly integrate with IaCM tools, deploying to a "Test" stage automatically triggers the creation of a corresponding "Test" environment. Once this environment is provisioned and configured with necessary details like IP addresses, passwords, and other environment-specific variables, the deployment and testing processes can proceed. Upon completion, the IaCM tool efficiently dismantles the environment, freeing up resources.

While this strategy offers significant benefits in terms of consistency, flexibility, and cost reduction, it's important to note that the environment creation and teardown process can add a few minutes to the overall test cycle. Therefore, ephemeral environments might not be the ideal solution for pipelines targeting extremely rapid delivery cadences, such as those measured in minutes. However, for delivery cycles measured in hours, days, or weeks, ephemeral environments provide a powerful way to break bottlenecks, improve consistency, and optimize infrastructure costs.

Summary

In this chapter we continued to navigate our delivery process, focusing on the continuous delivery steps that follow continuous integration. These are primarily testing steps, and we reviewed the types of tests that are important for validating all aspects of our software. We discussed the importance of reliable and predictable pre-production environments to testing and the best practices to give us these. By automating all aspects of promoting your release between testing stages, including promotion decision making, we can dramatically accelerate the delivery of our software.

After completing testing, there's only one step left to get our latest software release into the hands of users: actually deploying to production. We'll return to this step in Chapter 7. Before we get there, we'll take the next few chapters to discuss how we can fortify our releases to be more secure, more resilient, and more reliable.

CHAPTER 5

Securing Applications
and the Software Supply Chain

We've touched on security tools and practices throughout this book as we've navigated the delivery process from SCM to continuous integration and delivery. We discussed how RBAC and Policy-as-Code (PaC) governance in modern tools help secure your code repositories and pipelines, and we mentioned the role of early security testing in continuous integration. We looked at dynamic testing to uncover runtime vulnerabilities in your applications. This has been a light touch on security.

In this chapter, we'll bring security to the forefront and give it the attention it deserves in a world where cyberattacks are growing in both frequency and sophistication. High-profile breaches regularly make headlines, regulations are tightening globally, and customers increasingly evaluate vendors based on security posture.

With release cycles measured in days rather than months, the traditional model of security as a final gate before production has become untenable. Instead, we have shifted the burden "left" toward developers, who must now integrate security practices into their daily workflows. Developers who are not security experts now bear an unprecedented burden of security responsibility.

Artificial intelligence promises some relief for this tension. AI-powered security tools are improving detection accuracy, dramatically reducing false positives that waste developer time, and even automatically generating remediation code. Rather than simply shifting the security burden left, AI helps share that burden, providing developers with expert-level security guidance without requiring them to become security experts themselves.

This chapter will cover how the evolution toward AI-native software delivery has transformed how we approach security—not by simply adding more tools or processes, but by fundamentally changing how we identify, prioritize, and remediate security issues. We'll look at the importance of software supply chain security that is protecting the tools, processes, and people involved with how software is built and delivered, from the initial code to the final product. It's a critical concern as modern software relies heavily on interconnected components, each presenting potential vulnerabilities that could be exploited by malicious actors.

Understanding supply chain concerns and learning to evaluate your SDLC with a security lens will equip you to put strong security measures in place and better protect your applications, data, and your organization's reputation.

Modern Applications and the Cyberthreat Landscape

Building and deploying modern software applications relies heavily on distributed and complex software supply chains. These supply chains often encompass a vast network of code repositories, open source dependencies, third-party components, artifact repositories, and CI/CD pipelines. While this interconnectedness fosters innovation and accelerates our development cycles, it also introduces security risks throughout. The expanding attack surface and the potential for vulnerabilities to propagate throughout the supply chain have made our software supply chains a prime target for malicious actors.

In this section we'll look at these threats and learn how regulatory compliance frameworks that govern software supply chains are evolving to address them. Finally we'll look at how new compliance requirements impact your organization.

The Growing Threat of Software Supply Chain Attacks

The software supply chain encompasses all of the people, processes, and tools involved in creating and delivering software. It spans the complete lifecycle of software development, from the initial code creation to its deployment and maintenance. It's a complex ecosystem where each element plays a crucial role in the final product.

The software supply chain is made up of two primary concerns: applications and the DevOps toolchain, as shown in Figure 5-1.

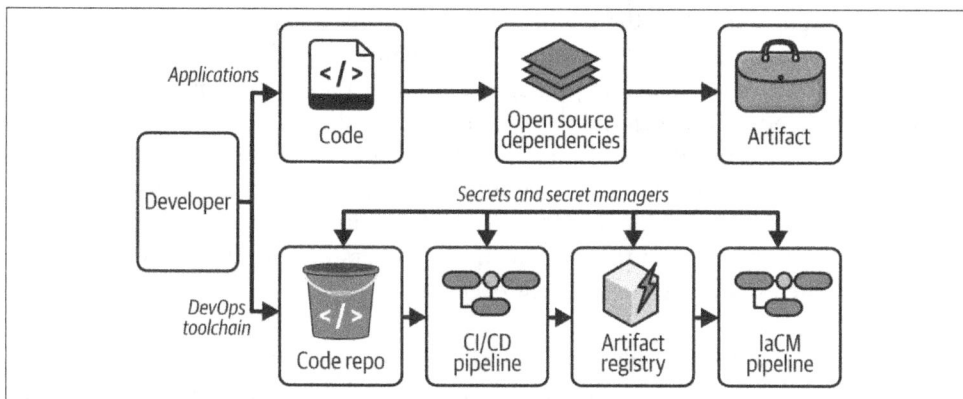

Figure 5-1. The software supply chain

Applications risks in the software supply chain

"Applications" here refers to all of the elements of your software, including your proprietary source code; open source dependencies like libraries, frameworks, and modules; and the software artifacts produced during the development process.

According to the 2024 Open Source Security and Risk Analysis report by Synopsys, 96% of codebases contain open source components. It's important to remember that our organizations are responsible for securing the open source components we use, just as they are with internally developed code. Because open source usage is so widespread, we shouldn't be surprised that over 80% of vulnerabilities found in applications are from OSS dependencies. A vulnerability discovered in 2021 in a widely used Java logging library called Log4j is an example of an open source–introduced threat. This vulnerability allowed attackers to remotely execute code on affected systems simply by sending a specially crafted string to the application's log. The exploit was exceptionally dangerous due to the widespread use of Log4j in applications and services, leading to a massive scramble to patch and mitigate the vulnerability.

The discovery of a backdoor in the widely used XZ Utils data compression tool provides another example. XZ Utils, like many OSS projects, is maintained by volunteers with limited resources for addressing security issues. One trusted contributor was found to have implemented a backdoor that would have allowed an attacker to gain administrator privileges to systems running software built with the tool. This utility is present in most Linux distributions, and was fortunately discovered before the tool had been widely deployed in production systems.

Another emerging threat in the application supply chain exploits the hallucinations of AI coding assistants. When AI models hallucinate package names, recommending nonexistent libraries or incorrect package identifiers, they create an opportunity for attackers. Malicious actors can monitor popular AI coding assistants for such hallucinations, and then register these hallucinated package names in public repositories. When developers attempt to use these nonexistent but AI-recommended packages, they unknowingly install malicious code. This "hallucination squatting" attack vector has already been observed in the wild, with researchers finding that common coding assistants frequently suggest nonexistent packages.

DevOps risks in the software supply chain

The DevOps toolchain includes the suite of tools and processes used to automate the building, testing, and deployment of your software. This encompasses code repositories, CI/CD tools and pipelines, artifact registries, and other tools that streamline the development process such as GitOps and IaCM tools.

The SolarWinds hack stands as a stark example of how a compromised DevOps toolchain can be exploited to propagate malicious code. In this sophisticated attack, threat actors infiltrated the SolarWinds Orion software build system, injecting malicious code into legitimate software updates. These tainted updates were then distributed to eighteen thousand SolarWinds customers, granting the attackers widespread access to their networks. This incident highlighted the potential for attackers to leverage the trust and automation inherent in DevOps pipelines to distribute malware at scale, turning a routine software update into a devastating cyberattack.

The Codecov supply chain hack in 2021 is another example of a toolchain security breach, one that impacted thousands of organizations. Malicious actors modified a Codecov Bash Uploader script (a tool customers use to upload code coverage data). This modification allowed the attackers to exfiltrate sensitive information, such as tokens, keys, and credentials from the continuous integration environments of Codecov's customers. The breach went undetected for over two months, potentially exposing sensitive data stored in customers' continuous integration environments.

A threat that is growing

Software supply chain attacks are not going away. Gartner Research (*https://oreil.ly/ Uwphu*) predicts that by 2025, 45% of organizations worldwide will have experienced attacks on their software supply chains. A security flaw in a line of code, a third-party library, or a tool in your pipeline can have a ripple effect, compromising the entire software product. Securing the software supply chain is about not just protecting individual components but also ensuring the integrity and security of the entire development and delivery process.

Regulatory Compliance Frameworks That Apply to Software Supply Chains

Given the increasing threat, governments and regulating authorities have responded with regulations that aim to address these challenges by establishing best practices, promoting transparency, and requiring organizations to take proactive measures to secure their software supply chains. Some of the most important compliance and regulatory frameworks that have emerged include the following:

United States Executive Order 14028, Improving the Nation's Cybersecurity
> This executive order, issued in 2021, mandates that federal agencies and their software providers enhance their software supply chain security practices. It emphasizes the use of secure software development practices, vulnerability disclosure, and incident response.

The European Union's Network and Information Security 2 Directive (NIS2 Directive)
> This directive aims to establish a high common level of cybersecurity across the EU. It includes provisions on software supply chain security, requiring organizations to assess and manage risks associated with software components and third-party dependencies.

NIST SP 800-218, Secure Software Development Framework (SSDF)
> This National Institute of Standards and Technology publication offers guidance for integrating security into the SDLC, including supply chain risk management. It provides a comprehensive framework for secure software development practices.

ISO/IEC 27036-2:2023
> This standard offers guidelines for managing information security risks related to suppliers and the supply chain. It covers various aspects, including supplier selection, contract management, and performance monitoring.

Payment Card Industry Data Security Standard (PCI DSS)
> While not solely focused on the software supply chain, PCI DSS requires organizations handling payment card data to implement secure software development practices, which include managing supply chain risks.

Cyber Resilience Act (CRA)
> This proposed EU regulation aims to enhance the cybersecurity of digital products and services. It includes requirements for vulnerability handling, security updates, software bill of materials (SBOM), and reporting actively exploited vulnerabilities within 24 hours of awareness.

In addition, Quality System Regulation (QSR) (21 CFR Part 820) and General Data Protection Regulation (GDPR) are frameworks that regulate software practices that indirectly impact software supply chain concerns. The QSR mandates rigorous controls and processes to ensure the safety and effectiveness of medical devices, encompassing software components. This includes requiring manufacturers to validate and control the software integrated into their devices. Similarly, GDPR's stringent requirements for protecting personal data necessitate that organizations implement robust technical and organizational measures, potentially extending to the security of software and its supply chain, especially if it processes personal data.

These frameworks and regulations contribute to a more secure and resilient software ecosystem, benefiting both businesses and consumers. However, the increased complexity can impact development teams. Understanding these requirements and integrating them into your processes is critical for successful compliance.

Securing Modern Applications with Shift Left

Against highly motivated hackers, our traditional wait-until-the-end security methods are not enough. Not only do these measures not provide the protection we require, but traditional security testing also slows the delivery of our software. To protect modern applications, organizations must use tools and practices designed for modern DevOps workflows. In this section we'll look at the challenges organizations face in implementing security practices. In Chapter 3 we touched on shift-left security, the practice of implementing security practices in the earliest stages of development. We'll look at how to use this approach to mitigate risks, as well as best practices for implementing shift-left security and managing vulnerabilities in a developer-friendly way.

The Need for Developer-Friendly Shift-Left Security

Rather than waiting until the end of the software development cycle to test the security of your application, you must actively address and test security concerns at every possible stage. This approach not only saves time and effort by avoiding extensive reworking of the software code later on but also enhances the overall security and efficiency of the final product. Figure 5-2 contrasts a shift-left security approach with a traditional application security approach.

It's important to note that effective shift-left security means more than performing security testing earlier in your delivery process. While this may help save developers from the cost of context switches that come when returning to code after days or weeks, it's ultimately not saving work. A truly effective implementation requires choosing security tools that seamlessly integrate with your CI/CD pipelines. These tools should not only identify vulnerabilities but also prioritize them based on severity and provide actionable insights. The tools you choose should normalize and de-duplicate findings, to help developers avoid alert fatigue and concentrate on the most critical risks. This integrated approach ensures that security is absolutely central to the development process.

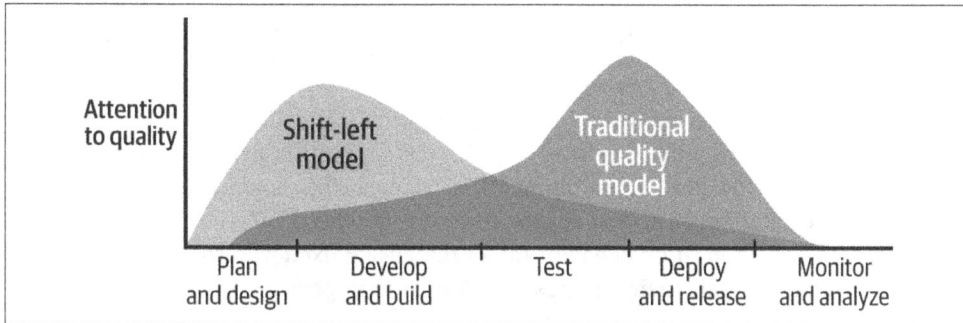

Figure 5-2. Shift-left approach contrasted with a traditional testing approach

Application Security Scanners

There are numerous scanners and tools available to do security testing and analysis, and many are now enhanced with AI capabilities. Let's look at the most common categories of these scanners and tools:

Software composition analysis (SCA)
> This type of scanner identifies vulnerabilities in third-party components and dependencies by analyzing software bills of materials (SBOMs) to detect known vulnerabilities in libraries and frameworks. We'll look at SBOMs later in this chapter. SCA tools feature significant ML capabilities around the likelihood a vulnerability can be reached or exploited. Snyk is one popular example of an SCA scanner.

Static application security testing (SAST)
> SAST tools analyze source code for potential vulnerabilities without executing the application by scanning code for patterns indicative of vulnerabilities, such as SQL injection, XSS, and buffer overflows. AI is enhancing SAST to reduce the incidence of false positives, wasting less engineer time. SonarQube, Checkmarx, and Fortify are examples of SAST tools.

Container scanning
> This type of scanning identifies vulnerabilities in container images and their dependencies by analyzing the contents of container images for known vulnerabilities and configuration errors.

Secret detection scanning
> This type of scanning detects sensitive information, such as API keys, passwords, and tokens, within code repositories and configuration files. With AI, secret detection tools are getting better at detecting obfuscated secrets and distinguishing between actual credentials and test data, reducing false positives and the associated toil.

Dynamic application security testing
> This testing method analyzes a running application to identify vulnerabilities by simulating external attacks. It interacts with the application like a real user to detect issues such as injection flaws, authentication problems, and configuration errors without needing access to the source code. AI-enhanced DAST tools generate test cases based on application behavior rather than using fixed patterns. They attempt to automatically validate their findings to tackle the false-positive problem.

Infrastructure-as-Code scanning
> This type of scan analyzes IaC files to identify security vulnerabilities, misconfigurations, and compliance issues before deployment.

These types of scanners are integrated early in software development pipelines, in line with the shift-left approach. Secret scanning is a recommended security practice that automatically identifies and alerts users to sensitive information in code repositories and other data sources.

This prevents sensitive information from being incorporated into a codebase to begin with. SCA tools are also typically integrated early in the pipeline, after code is committed and before building. SAST scans can be part of a build phase. Container scanning is typically integrated after container images are built and before deployment.

By incorporating SCA, SAST, container scanning, secret scanning, DAST, and IaC scanning throughout your development pipelines, you can effectively implement shift-left security and proactively protect your applications from vulnerabilities.

Every issue that your test tools identify must be triaged. There is cost in reviewing the issue, determining if it is real or not, and then remediating it. False positives, issues that are reported but are not real, are a significant problem. They waste the time of the reviewer, draining resources from other security efforts and innovation. Further, by "crying wolf" they diminish the trust engineers place in security findings, and can slow response times to other, real problems. With this in mind, it's no surprise that reducing the number of false positives is a key priority for AI in many scanning tools.

The triage problem is exacerbated by the number of scanners involved, which may find the same issues in different ways. In some organizations, there may even be multiple SAST tools used on the same codebase. In these environments, security test orchestration layers may be used to de-duplicate and normalize the findings into a single, manageable list. In an AI-native environment, AI/ML has a role to play here in pattern-matching as well as reducing developer toil.

Issues will be detected across all these types of scanners and need to be remediated. Security tools are increasingly offering automated or semi-automated remediation through specialized AI coding assistants to streamline this process for developers.

Securing the Software Supply Chain

In this section we'll examine common security risks inherent to today's software supply chains. We'll look at risks associated with code repositories, CI/CD pipelines, artifact repositories, open source dependencies, and the infrastructure underpinning your software development process. AI is transforming how organizations detect and respond to these risks by identifying patterns and anomalies across complex supply chains that would be impossible to monitor manually at scale. We'll look at various frameworks and benchmarks you can use to assess the security of your toolchain. By the end of this section, you'll have a better understanding of the potential threats and how to mitigate them.

The complexity of modern software supply chains creates an ideal use case for artificial intelligence. AI systems can continuously monitor for suspicious patterns across repositories, build systems, and deployments. For example, ML models can detect unusual commit patterns that might indicate a compromised developer account, identify suspicious package behavior that signals a potential supply chain attack, or spot configuration drifts that could create security vulnerabilities. These AI capabilities provide unprecedented visibility and protection across interconnected components.

Identifying Top CI/CD Security Risks

The Open Worldwide Application Security Project (OWASP), a leading organization focused on improving software security, has identified the top 10 CI/CD security risks. As the following list illustrates, the range of threats are diverse. Understanding these risks and implementing the recommended mitigation strategies will help you secure and strengthen your CI/CD ecosystem:

Insufficient flow control mechanisms
> Insufficient flow control mechanisms in CI/CD pipelines can be exploited by attackers who can gain access to your pipeline. By bypassing necessary reviews and approvals, malicious code or artifacts can be pushed through the pipeline, potentially reaching production environments with severe consequences.

Inadequate identity and access management
> The complexity of managing numerous identities across various systems, combined with the tendency for overly permissive accounts, can lead to compromise. If any user account is compromised, attackers could gain extensive access, potentially reaching the production environment.

Dependency chain abuse

Dependency chain abuse refers to the exploitation of vulnerabilities in how your development and build systems fetch code dependencies. This can happen when these systems are tricked into fetching and executing malicious packages instead of legitimate ones. Attackers exploit it by publishing malicious packages with the same name as internal packages (dependency confusion), hijacking maintainer accounts (dependency hijacking), or relying on typos (typosquatting) to trick developers into downloading their packages.

Poisoned pipeline execution

This is a cyberattack where malicious code is injected into a CI/CD pipeline, often through compromised source control systems. The poisoned code can then be executed within the pipeline, potentially granting attackers the same access and privileges as the build job. The attacker can manipulate build configuration files or other files the pipeline relies on, leading to actions such as credential theft, data exfiltration, or deployment of malicious artifacts.

Insufficient pipeline-based access controls

The risk arises when pipeline execution nodes have excessive access to resources and systems. This can be exploited by attackers to run malicious code within a pipeline, abusing the permissions granted to the pipeline to move laterally within or outside the CI/CD system.

Insufficient credential hygiene

Insufficient credential hygiene is a significant risk in environments where credentials are widely used across different systems and contexts. Examples include accidental code pushes containing credentials, insecure usage in build and deployment processes, unrotated credentials, and credentials being printed to console outputs or stored within container images.

Insecure system configuration

Insecure system configuration is a common vulnerability due to the numerous systems and vendors in a typical toolchain. Misconfigurations, such as outdated software, overly permissive access controls, or insecure default settings, can easily be exploited by attackers to gain unauthorized access, manipulate CI/CD flows, or even compromise production environments.

Ungoverned usage of third-party services

Third-party services in CI/CD pipelines, while convenient and valuable for development, can easily be granted excessive access to sensitive resources, effectively expanding the attack surface of an organization. This lack of governance and visibility makes it difficult to maintain proper access controls, leaving organizations vulnerable to attacks if any of these third-party services are compromised.

Improper artifact integrity validation

Due to the multiple stages and sources involved in software delivery, malicious actors can potentially tamper with artifacts without raising alarms. If not detected, these compromised artifacts can flow through the pipeline and eventually be deployed into production, executing malicious code and compromising systems.

Insufficient logging and visibility

Without robust logging, you're essentially blind to malicious activities happening within your development pipeline, making it difficult to detect and respond to attacks in a timely manner.

Understanding these risks and implementing the recommended mitigation strategies is key to building a secure and resilient CI/CD ecosystem.

Identifying Top OSS Risks

OSS dependency usage is ubiquitous, and so organizations must contend with the security and compliance risks that it brings. We previously mentioned two examples. In the first, the Log4j threat, thousands of systems were impacted. The second, the XZ Utils example, while caught early, illustrated how a malicious actor could wreak havoc by compromising an OSS component.

Common vulnerabilities and exposures (CVEs) are one mechanism that organizations can use to identify known security problems in order to take steps to mitigate them. CVE monitoring tools automate the process of scanning your software and alerting you to the potential risks. While diligent monitoring can help you eliminate known threats from the OSS you use, it does not guarantee that your OSS components are truly safe. Unmaintained components or outdated dependencies also create risks, and because OSS packages bring in dozens of dependencies, these can be very complex to manage.

While CVE management can help fight known threats, there are other classes of threats to contend with. The OWASP Foundation has created the following top 10 list to capture a fuller spectrum of OSS risks that your organization needs to guard against:

Known vulnerabilities

An open source component can contain security flaws that are publicly disclosed, often through CVEs or other channels. These vulnerabilities, if exploitable in your software, can compromise your system's confidentiality, integrity, or availability.

Compromise of legitimate package

Attackers may inject malicious code into existing projects or distribution infrastructure by hijacking accounts or exploiting vulnerabilities. This can lead to code execution on end user or organizational systems, putting confidentiality, integrity, and availability at risk.

Name confusion attacks

Name confusion attacks involve malicious actors creating components with names that closely resemble legitimate ones, aiming to trick users into installing them. These attacks can lead to the execution of harmful code on both user and organizational systems, compromising confidentiality, integrity, and availability.

Unmaintained software

Because unmaintained OSS components are no longer actively developed or supported, patches for new vulnerabilities might not be available. This situation can result in increased effort and longer resolution times for downstream developers who need to create their own patches.

Outdated software

Using outdated software components in your projects can create significant challenges. It can make emergency updates difficult, especially if vulnerabilities are discovered in the version you're using. Older releases also may not be as thoroughly tested for security issues as newer versions.

Untracked dependencies

Untracked dependencies can introduce vulnerabilities without the developers' knowledge. These dependencies may be missed due to incomplete SBOMs, limited SCA tool capabilities, or manual installation methods.

License risk

Open source components may have licenses that are incompatible with the intended use, violate legal requirements, or lack a license altogether. Using components without a license or failing to comply with license terms can lead to legal repercussions.

Immature software

Immature open source projects, lacking best practices like standard versioning, testing, or documentation, can introduce operational risks to your software. This lack of maturity may lead to unexpected behavior and increased development effort along with vulnerabilities.

Unapproved change

Unapproved changes to software components can lead to compromised integrity and reproducibility of software builds.

Under-/oversized dependency

> Open source components can vary significantly in size and functionality, leading to security risks. Small components offer minimal functionality but can still introduce significant risk due to their reliance on upstream projects. Large components, while potentially offering more features, may have a larger attack surface due to unused capabilities and dependencies.

In the next section we'll look at a framework—SLSA—that can help address these risks.

Ensuring Integrity with Supply Chain Levels for Software Artifacts

Clearly, the risks of OSS are numerous. Before we leverage OSS or any third-party components in our own software, we must ask: Who wrote this software? Was it built and released with tools and on platforms that we can trust? What dependencies does it bring in? Does it conform to the regulatory requirements that are important to us?

Supply Chain Levels for Software Artifacts (SLSA, pronounced "salsa") is a framework that provides a structured approach to answering these questions. SLSA is designed to bolster the integrity of software artifacts throughout the software supply chain. It enhances the security of software supply chains and can help address the OSS threats we've looked at.

Similar to the chain of custody for physical evidence, SLSA emphasizes the importance of tracking and verifying the integrity of software artifacts throughout their lifecycle. In this section, we'll dig into SLSA and provide guidance on how to comply with its requirements to safeguard your software from potential threats.

SLSA Overview

SLSA is an open source project driven by the Open Source Security Foundation. With its focus on practical implementation and measurable security improvements, SLSA has gained significant traction.

SLSA offers benefits to providers and consumers of OSS and vendor-provided software. Within your organization you can use SLSA to help secure your software development process from internal tampering. This ensures that the code that you deploy to production is the code you've built, tested, and signed off on.

For consumers of software, SLSA provides mechanisms to verify the authenticity and integrity of OSS. Package registries are able to use SLSA to guarantee that an uploaded OSS package is built from a source in a legitimate repository. As an OSS consumer, sourcing from trusted registries ensures the packages you download are valid. In addition, you can require that your vendors adhere to SLSA principles.

Verifying vendor SLSA certifications from reputable third-party auditors can provide an extra layer of confidence.

SLSA defines a tiered framework (*https://oreil.ly/i7qar*), allowing organizations to progressively enhance their software supply chain security. Levels represent increasing degrees of assurance and protection against tampering. An organization with no protections in place is considered at Level 0.

SLSA Level 1 is the foundation. Level 1 requires that basic provenance information be produced. This information should detail the build processes, describe dependencies, and give the source code location. Level 1 is the starting point for organizations embarking on their software supply chain security journey. Consumers can use this information to make decisions about the risks associated with the software.

Level 2 builds upon Level 1 by introducing stronger build requirements. Your build environment must be isolated and controlled. This level also mandates artifact signing for integrity verification, preventing tampering.

Finally, Level 3 requires source code provenance and build reproducibility. Provenance must be auditable and its integrity must be ensured.

Table 5-1 summarizes requirements at each of the three levels SLSA 1.0 defines.

Table 5-1. SLSA levels

Implementer	Requirement	Degree	L1	L2	L3
Producer	Choose an appropriate build platform		✓	✓	✓
	Follow a consistent build process		✓	✓	✓
	Distribute provenance		✓	✓	✓
Build platform	Provence generation exists	Exists	✓	✓	✓
	Provence generation is ensured to be authentic	Authentic		✓	✓
	Provence generation is unforgeable	Unforgeable			✓
	Isolation strength	Hosted		✓	✓
	Isolation strength	Isolated			✓

Using SLSA to Ensure Integrity

The following principles have guided the design decisions of the SLSA framework:

Trust a small number of platforms; focus on artifacts
   Extend trust to a few core platforms, such as build and packaging tools, and then automate the verification of artifacts produced by those platforms. For example, your trusted build platform produces and signs provenance attestations for each artifact it's used to build. Downstream platforms then verify the provenance signed by the public key to automatically determine that an artifact meets the SLSA level.

Trace software back to source code, not individuals

Establish a direct and verifiable link between the final software artifact and its original source code. This approach is in contrast with trusting individuals with write access to package registries and trusting the immutable and analyzable nature of code itself. By establishing a direct link, organizations can significantly reduce the risk of malicious code injection or unauthorized modifications.

Prefer attestations over inferences

Rely on direct evidence of an artifact's origin over inferring the trustworthiness of the artifact based on knowledge of intermediary build systems or other systems. Instead of inferring the integrity, SLSA mandates explicit attestations about an artifact's provenance. This requires concrete proof of an artifact's build process.

In SLSA 1.0, the build platform is central to ensuring artifact integrity. *Build platform* is used to refer to the systems responsible for compiling, packaging, and preparing your software for distribution. A robust build platform is essential for achieving higher SLSA levels. The system you select should support isolated builds, meaning for each build, new infrastructure is created, and after the build runs, the infrastructure is deleted. In addition, the system should enforce nonprivileged, containerized continuous integration steps that do not use volume mounts. This prevents access to the provenance key information in compliance with SLSA specifications. With a fortified build system, you are assured that malicious actors can't tamper with your build.

In addition to choosing a build platform that can guarantee artifact integrity, your system should produce and distribute attestations (digitally signed records) that demonstrate that your software meets your desired SLSA build level. SLSA provenance attestations are cryptographic signatures that provide verifiable evidence about the origin and build process of a software artifact. They act as a digital passport, ensuring the integrity and authenticity of the artifact.

Consider a container image built using a CI/CD pipeline. An SLSA provenance attestation for this image might include the following information:

Builder

The CI/CD platform used to build the image (e.g., GitHub Actions, GitLab CI/CD)

Invocation

The specific build configuration or script used to create the image

Materials

The source code repositories, dependencies, and other inputs used in the build process

Subject
> The artifact itself, identified by its unique digest (hash)

Signature
> A cryptographic signature generated by a trusted entity, verifying the authenticity and integrity of the attestation

To validate SLSA provenance attestations, organizations can use tools like the SLSA Verifier Service. This service verifies the authenticity of the attestation, checks the signature against the public key of the trusted signer, and ensures the attestation adheres to the SLSA specification.

To achieve maximum security, SLSA recommends that build platforms, rather than individual developers, generate provenance. If your organization doesn't use a build platform, consider adopting one with SLSA support. For third-party platforms, check their compatibility and request SLSA support if needed. If you maintain your own build platform, add SLSA provenance generation capabilities.

Similarly, package ecosystems should distribute SLSA provenance alongside software packages, embedding attestations within packages or providing them as separate metadata files. If your organization uses a third-party ecosystem, inquire about SLSA support and follow their guidelines. For direct distribution, include SLSA provenance within your package artifacts.

By leveraging SLSA provenance attestations, your organization can gain confidence in the authenticity and integrity of software artifacts and reduce the risk of supply chain attacks.

Enhancing supply chain security beyond SLSA

While SLSA provides an excellent framework for build integrity, it primarily focuses on artifact provenance and build system integrity. To address the full spectrum of supply chain risks identified in the OWASP Top Ten CI/CD risks, organizations need additional security measures.

A comprehensive supply chain security strategy should include:

Continuous behavioral monitoring
> Modern delivery and security platforms, powered by AI and ML, are improving to detect anomalous activities across repositories, build systems, and deployment pipelines. These systems establish baselines of normal behavior and flag deviations that might indicate compromise. Monitoring and security tools such as Datadog CI and GitGuardian are popular choices today.

Advanced dependency analysis

Beyond basic vulnerability scanning, intelligent analysis tools can evaluate package behavior, code patterns, and maintainer activity trends to identify potentially malicious dependencies before they're publicly reported. AI-powered systems can detect subtle indicators of compromise by analyzing code semantics and behavior in ways that traditional scanners cannot, helping to protect against sophisticated supply chain attacks like dependency confusion or typosquatting.

Automated policy enforcement

Implement automated policy guardrails throughout your pipelines that enforce security requirements beyond build integrity. These systems prevent overly permissive access, block dangerous configurations, and ensure proper secrets management—addressing risks like insufficient RBAC and credential hygiene that SLSA doesn't fully cover. Today, implementing policy widely across a delivery platform is still unevenly done. Looking forward, it is a strong approach and one that will benefit from AI both in becoming more adaptable to changing threats and in rapid creation of policy through AI code generation assistance in PaC scenarios.

Supply chain risk prediction

Predictive analytics and AI models analyze historical vulnerability trends and emerging threat intelligence to highlight components in your supply chain that pose higher potential risk, helping teams proactively address vulnerabilities before they become critical issues. By analyzing patterns across thousands of projects and dependencies, these systems identify risk factors in your environment before they lead to security incidents, enabling proactive hardening of vulnerable areas.

By combining these AI-enhanced capabilities with SLSA's build integrity focus, organizations can create a defense-in-depth approach that addresses the full range of supply chain risks. This comprehensive strategy protects not just the build process but also the entire software delivery pipeline, from development through deployment.

Addressing AI-generated dependency risks

As organizations increasingly adopt AI coding assistants, a new supply chain risk has emerged: AI hallucination squatting. This occurs when attackers register package names that AI tools incorrectly suggest through hallucinations, creating a vector for malicious code injection.

While the core SLSA framework provides significant protection against traditional supply chain attacks, organizations using AI coding tools should implement additional safeguards:

Verified registry policies

Configure package managers to only pull from officially vetted registries and private repositories with known-good packages. This prevents developers from inadvertently installing packages from untrusted sources, even if an AI assistant suggests them.

Package age and popularity checks

Implement tooling that automatically verifies recommended packages against minimum download counts and established history metrics. New packages with minimal usage should trigger additional review.

AI confidence verification

When using AI coding assistants that provide confidence scores for their recommendations, implement processes to flag low-confidence package suggestions for manual verification against authoritative sources.

Preinstallation validation

Add automated checks to your development environment that validate package existence and provenance in trusted repositories before allowing dependencies to be added to project files.

These additional controls, when combined with SLSA practices and comprehensive SBOMs, create a defense-in-depth approach that protects against both traditional supply chain attacks and emerging AI-facilitated threats. By addressing the specific risks that AI introduces to the dependency selection process, organizations can safely leverage AI coding assistants while maintaining supply chain integrity. With the exception of AI confidence verification, each of these practices is helpful against other package-based attacks, such as typosquatting.

Addressing Zero-Day Vulnerabilities with Software Bill of Materials

In the first section, we looked at the Log4j exploit that allowed attackers to execute arbitrary code remotely by exploiting a specific pattern in log messages, leading to widespread data breaches, ransomware attacks, and disruptions to critical services. This was an example of a zero-day exploit, one of the most insidious types of threats because it exploits vulnerabilities that are unknown to the software vendor, giving attackers a significant advantage before any defenses can be put in place. In this section, we'll look at how an SBOM serves as an essential tool in the battle against this type of vulnerability. An SBOM provides a detailed inventory of all components and dependencies used in a software artifact. We'll look at the composition and characteristics of SBOMs, and how they are managed throughout the SDLC.

While dependency management tools and package managers have existed for years to track and manage software components, SBOM has witnessed significant advancements since 2018. Collaborative efforts, including the National Telecommunications and Information Administration (NTIA) Multistakeholder Process, have developed best practices and recommendations for SBOMs. This collaborative effort brought together industry experts, government agencies, and academics to define standards and guidelines for SBOM generation, sharing, and consumption.

As a result, SBOM has emerged as a key building block. In fact, recent Linux Foundation research (*https://oreil.ly/allVL*) found that 78% of organizations were producing or consuming SBOMs in 2022, up 66% from the prior year.

You have two standards to choose from when creating SBOMs for your software:

CycloneDX
> The CycloneDX project emerged as a leading standard for SBOMs, providing a machine-readable format for representing software components, dependencies, and their relationships. CycloneDX has gained widespread adoption and support from various organizations.

SPDX
> Software Package Data Exchange (SPDX) is another popular standard for SBOMs, sponsored by the Linux Foundation and codified in the ISO/IEC 5962 international standard. It offers a flexible and extensible format for representing software components. SPDX has been widely used in the open source community for many years.

SPDX is a more established format with a broader scope, encompassing not only component information but also metadata about the SBOM itself, such as its creator and creation date. It's particularly well-suited for managing OSS licenses and sharing information about packages.

CycloneDX is a newer format that offers a more structured and machine-readable approach, with a focus on providing detailed information about software components and their relationships. CycloneDX is often preferred for its flexibility and adaptability, making it suitable for a wide range of use cases. Your specific use case may determine which standard you adopt; the tools and processes you select for software supply chain security management should be able to support both standards.

Regardless of the specific format you choose, the factors you use to assess the quality of the SBOM are the same. The NTIA has developed a set of minimum elements that SBOMs should contain to provide essential information about software components and their dependencies. Ensuring the presence of these elements will facilitate effective analysis of SBOMs across various tools and platforms, as well as adherence to the underlying SPDX or CycloneDX specification.

By providing a comprehensive inventory of components, SBOMs offer transparency and traceability that can help ensure compliance with your organization's security policies and legal requirements. PaC frameworks can leverage SBOMs to automate this compliance. With PaC you define security policies using code, which can be managed and version-controlled like code. These policies can then be applied to SBOMs, ensuring that software components adhere to the organization's security standards for OSS. Automated compliance reduces the risk of human error and improves efficiency.

For example, your organization might define a policy that only allows OSS components with permissive licenses (e.g., MIT, Apache License 2.0) to be used to ensure compatibility with the organization's existing software portfolio and avoid potential legal issues.

You might define a policy to automatically reject OSS components with known vulnerabilities above a certain severity threshold. Or you could establish criteria for evaluating the reputation and trustworthiness of OSS vendors. This can include factors like vendor size, security practices, and community involvement.

Combining SBOMs with PaC creates a powerful framework for governing OSS usage, ensuring compliance, and mitigating security risks. Automating enforcement of security policies reduces the burden on security teams and improves overall efficiency.

Using SBOMs to Remediate Dependency Issues

In complex codebases with countless dependencies, pinpointing and fixing affected artifacts can be a daunting task. Adhering to the following best practices can help your organization be ready to react quickly to zero-day exploits and other threats:

Keep SBOMs up-to-date
Ensure that SBOMs are generated automatically as part of your CI/CD processes. This ensures that you always have up-to-date information about your software's dependencies for every artifact your organization supports.

Utilize automated vulnerability scanning tools
Employ automated tools to scan your SBOMs against vulnerability databases. These tools can identify known vulnerabilities in your dependencies in a timely way, allowing you to prioritize remediation efforts and address potential security threats.

Establish a robust patch management process
Develop a well-defined process for patching vulnerabilities identified in your SBOMs. This includes setting priorities for patching, coordinating with vendors, and testing patches before deployment. By maintaining an up-to-date and secure software supply chain, you can significantly reduce the risk of zero-day exploits being used.

AI significantly enhances these best practices. Intelligent SBOM analysis systems can:

Predict vulnerability impact
> AI models can analyze your application architecture to determine if a vulnerable component is in an exploitable position, distinguishing between theoretical vulnerabilities and those that pose immediate risk. This contextual analysis helps teams focus on the most critical issues first.

Automate dependency updates
> When vulnerabilities are identified, AI systems can automatically generate pull requests with appropriate dependency updates, test compatibility with your codebase, and manage the update process across multiple repositories. This automation dramatically reduces the time from vulnerability disclosure to remediation.

Identify hidden dependencies
> ML algorithms can detect undocumented or transitive dependencies that might not be explicitly captured in package manifests, providing a more complete view of your actual attack surface.

Adopting DevSecOps Principles

We've seen in this chapter how vulnerable the software supply chain is. Consistently delivering software in a secure manner requires more than careful vetting of the tools and third-party components that you use. It requires more than choosing CI/CD tools and technologies that support SLSA and the generation of SBOMs and attestations. To ensure consistent secure delivery, your team must maintain a secure platform, conduct thorough vulnerability testing, prioritize and fix issues promptly, prevent insecure code releases, comply with regulations, and guarantee the integrity of your software and all of its components.

This cannot be the work of a single role on your team or a single team within your organization. It requires a collaborative approach that integrates security into the entire SDLC. This is what a DevSecOps approach speaks to. Unlike traditional approaches where security is added on in a few places, DevSecOps promotes continual collaboration between development, security, and operations teams, ensuring that security is considered from the beginning.

In this section, we'll explain DevSecOps principles and show how adopting these principles will help you to more quickly identify and remediate vulnerabilities, reduce the risk of breaches, and improve the overall security of your software.

Establish a Collaborative Culture and Break Down Functional Silos

The first and most vital step to successfully implementing DevSecOps is to establish a collaborative culture with a security-first mindset. Naturally, this can be the most difficult step and requires the full support of your organization's leadership team. Security must be an organizational priority and become a responsibility shared by developers, operations, security teams, and others.

A simple way to break down silos and establish a shared sense of ownership is to create cross-functional DevSecOps teams. Siloed teams can limit communication and knowledge sharing, which can lead to duplicated efforts and inconsistent processes. In contrast, cross-functional DevSecOps teams foster collaboration and open communication. By including the perspective of development, operations, and security roles when, for example, establishing a new security practice or selecting a new security-related tool, you can more easily get the buy-in and alignment needed to be successful.

In addition, cross-functional teams can help prevent selections or recommendations that create bottlenecks and strain productivity. An example of this would be a unilateral mandate to impose some new application security checks without considering their impact on the development process. The impact of this would be increased workload for developers, which strains not only productivity but also the trust and goodwill within your organization.

In addition to creating cross-functional teams, you should identify and support a few key security champions across your organization to help promote security initiatives and raise awareness among their peers. Use your cross-functional teams and security champions to share ideas and communicate your progress by establishing open and transparent communication channels to facilitate the exchange of information and ideas. This can include regular meetings, team chats, and knowledge-sharing sessions.

AI tools serve as collaborative bridges between security and development teams by providing shared context and translating between security and development concerns. For example, when an AI-powered security tool identifies a vulnerability, it can explain the issue in developer-friendly terms while also providing the security context that security teams need. This shared understanding reduces friction between teams and helps establish a security culture where everyone speaks the same language.

Lastly, invest in security training. Identify skills gaps and provide ongoing security training to all team members, equipping them with the knowledge and skills to identify and mitigate security risks. This not only raises the bar of the entire team, but also demonstrates your organizational commitment to security as a priority.

Adopt and Enforce Secure Coding Methodologies and Shift-Left

Secure coding practices are essential for preventing vulnerabilities. The OWASP Top 10 and Common Weakness Enumeration (CWE) provide helpful guidance for identifying and addressing common security vulnerabilities. In addition, ensure your methodologies address the following common threats:

Input validation
> Always validate user input to prevent malicious data from being injected into your application. This can help prevent SQL injection, XSS, and other injection attacks.

Output encoding
> Properly encode output to prevent XSS attacks. This ensures that user-generated content is displayed safely on the page without allowing malicious code to be executed.

Error handling
> Implement robust error handling to prevent information leakage and potential vulnerabilities. Avoid displaying sensitive error messages that could provide attackers with valuable information.

Session management
> Use secure session management techniques to protect user data and prevent unauthorized access. This includes using strong session identifiers and implementing timeouts.

Authentication and authorization
> Implement strong authentication mechanisms and enforce proper authorization controls to restrict access to sensitive resources.

Cryptography
> Use secure cryptographic algorithms and practices to protect sensitive data. Avoid weak encryption methods and ensure proper key management.

Dependency management
> Keep dependencies up-to-date and manage them securely to avoid vulnerabilities. Use tools like dependency scanners to identify and address known vulnerabilities in third-party libraries.

While staying informed about the latest threats and secure coding can prevent many vulnerabilities, your organization's best efforts won't be infallible. Static and dynamic analysis tools, along with early-stage security testing, act as a backstop, catching issues that might be overlooked in code reviews. This is where shift-left comes in. We've covered how shift-left enables you to identify and address vulnerability at an early stage. Early remediation reduces the risk of vulnerabilities getting released into production code.

Summary

Security cannot be an afterthought in modern software development. It must be an integral part of the entire development process. As we've seen throughout this chapter, an AI-native approach to security transforms:

- How vulnerabilities are discovered, using intelligent analysis rather than just static rules
- How findings are prioritized, based on actual risk rather than generic severity ratings
- How remediations are implemented, with automated guidance and code generation
- How supply chains are secured, through continuous monitoring and anomaly detection
- How teams collaborate, with shared context and understanding across security and development

By embedding security into every phase, from design to deployment, and by fostering a culture of shared responsibility augmented by AI, organizations can build and deliver applications that are fortified against modern threats.

In Chapter 6, we'll turn our attention to making our apps more resilient by using chaos testing to uncover weaknesses that might otherwise go undetected.

Chaos Engineering and Service Reliability

Complex modern systems are inherently vulnerable. Even seemingly minor disruptions, or a single weak link, can cause issues that spiral to have catastrophic consequences.

Consider this scenario: a prominent e-commerce platform suffers a significant outage during a peak sales event, comparable to Black Friday. As traffic builds, the platform's checkout service grinds to a crawl, eventually culminating in complete failure. Thousands of customers are left unable to finalize purchases, resulting in not only immediate lost revenue but also damaged reputation and eroded trust and brand loyalty. Postincident analysis reveals the root cause to be network latency between the checkout service and a critical pricing data cache. As the cache response slowed under the strain of high traffic, the system's retry mechanism became overwhelmed, leading to a cascade of failed requests that ultimately overloaded the database.

Scenarios like these and the rising cost of failures have led to the emergence of service reliability as a discipline and the practice of chaos engineering (sometimes called failure or fault injection testing). The goal of chaos engineering is to provide an understanding of how systems behave when stressed in an unusual (chaotic) way. The increased popularity of these practices has been fueled by the development of new tools, technologies, and practices.

The term chaos engineering can be traced back to Netflix in 2010. The company was transitioning its infrastructure to the cloud, which introduced new complexity, with hundreds of microservices interacting in unpredictable ways. To test the resilience of their systems, Netflix engineers developed Chaos Monkey, a tool designed to randomly terminate VM instances in their production environment. This simulated real-world failures, forcing engineers to build systems that could gracefully handle unexpected disruptions.

The use of the word chaos and the image of a monkey set loose to randomly terminate software in a production environment does conjure mayhem. Given these preconceptions, introducing chaos engineering into an organization may be met with resistance. More than one boss has wondered, "Don't we have enough chaos around here?"

In this chapter, we'll counter those notions by understanding modern chaos engineering as a rigorous approach to implementing experiments. As a methodology, we use this *controlled* disruption to test the resilience of our systems. In addition to testing our current state, chaos engineering gives us a powerful methodology to systematically improve resilience.

The experiments we conduct give us a deeper understanding of our software's behavior under stress. This knowledge enables us to design targeted improvements. We then test to validate their effectiveness in meeting our targets.

Service Reliability and Service Resiliency

Service reliability and service resiliency are related concepts. The former is the probability that a service will perform its intended function without failure for a specified period under defined conditions. The latter is the ability of a service to withstand and recover from disruptions, such as hardware failures, software bugs, network outages, or even cyberattacks. It's about how well a service can bounce back from adversity.

While distinct, they are interconnected. A highly reliable service is less likely to experience failures, but even the most reliable systems can encounter unexpected problems. That's where resiliency comes in. It ensures that even when failures occur, the service can recover quickly and minimize disruptions to users.

We'll also cover how to use service-level objectives (SLOs) to set our resiliency targets. We'll look at using error budgets to allow for an acceptable level of failure within that target. We'll see how chaos engineering works with these mechanisms by helping us validate whether our system can operate within its error budget and still meet our targets even when facing unexpected disruptions.

In this chapter we'll also move beyond static chaos experiments to understand a more modern and dynamic approach that involves integrating chaos engineering into our CI/CD pipelines, allowing us to continuously assess and improve system resilience as part of our regular development workflows.

Throughout this chapter, we will explore how advanced chaos engineering tools leverage AI/ML-driven insights to recommend and guide the execution of these experiments, leading to more efficient and effective resilience testing while reducing risk. We will also see how agentic AI, GenAI, and MCP address critical scalability and precision challenges in chaos engineering by automating experiment design, enabling

---

dynamic risk detection, and providing intelligent remediation. These technologies transform chaos engineering from a reactive practice into a proactive, self-optimizing system resilience strategy.

Getting Started with Chaos Engineering

While many chaos engineering experiments employ randomness (e.g., selecting a random server or service to take down), the practice of chaos engineering is as methodical as lab science. In this section, we'll dive into the core tenets of chaos engineering and look at best practices to reduce the risk of causing service disruptions when conducting experiments.

Principles of Chaos Engineering

Netflix has defined a set of core principles that provide a useful framework for exploring how your systems behave under stress. A structured approach ensures that your chaos experiments are not just disruptive events but structured investigations that generate valuable data that you can use to drive improvements to your system's resilience. These principles are:

Defining a "steady state" that characterizes normal system behavior
Observability is key here. You must have the metrics you need to understand the normal range of values that indicate your system is healthy and performing as expected. This could include request latency, error rates, throughput, or application-specific metrics. Be sure to account for external factors that might influence your metrics, such as time of day, day of week, or the presence of a marketing campaign that could spike traffic.

Turning expectation into a hypothesis
Based on your understanding of the system's architecture and dependencies, formulate a hypothesis about how it *should* behave when a specific failure is introduced. Frame your hypothesis in a way that can be objectively tested using your chosen metrics. For example, "If we simulate a 20% increase in traffic, the average response time should remain below three seconds, and the error rate should not exceed 0.5%."

Executing the experiment by simulating real-world events
Use chaos engineering tools to automate the injection of failures. Simulate a server crashing or becoming unavailable, an outage of a critical third-party service, or a sudden surge in user requests.

Evaluating the results against the hypothesis
    Compare the system's behavior during the experiment to your established base-line and your hypothesized outcome. Did the metrics stay within acceptable ranges? Did the system recover as expected? Were any unexpected side effects observed? If the system deviates from the expected behavior, investigate the root cause. Based on the experiment's outcome, refine your hypotheses and adjust your system design or operational procedures to enhance resilience.

Starting Small and Scaling

Simulating failures to intentionally take down systems does, of course, incur risk. We knowingly incur risk in this controlled way to validate the hypothesis we've defined. An important strategy for reducing risk is to start with small experiments.

To illustrate starting small and scaling experiments, let's walk through an example focused on testing a checkout service in an e-commerce system. This service is a critical microservice that processes user purchases. The expected outcome is simple: a customer adds items to their cart, proceeds to checkout, and completes the payment. The customer expects a smooth, fast, and reliable experience.

Behind the scenes, this straightforward operation relies on a series of complex processes. The checkout service depends on multiple APIs and external services to function properly, including inventory systems, payment gateways, and caching layers (like Redis) to quickly retrieve important data such as product prices, discounts, and availability. The checkout service fetches pricing data from a cache for quick access. If the cache is slow or fails, the checkout service should still provide the right information by failing over to another cache instance or even to a database as a backup, though it may be slower.

> GenAI can transform chaos engineering from manual hypothesis testing into an adaptive, self-optimizing resilience validation system. This approach proves particularly valuable in critical e-commerce workflows like checkout services, where balancing risk mitigation with realistic failure simulation is paramount.

Developers typically configure retry logic, timeouts, and circuit breakers to handle network issues or failures. Let's look at each:

Retry logic
    This ensures that if a request to the cache fails or experiences network issues, the system will automatically try again a few times before giving up. This helps handle transient failures. The system might, for example, retry up to three times with a delay of 100 ms between each retry.

Timeouts

Timeout settings define how long the service should wait for a response before deciding that the attempt has failed. This prevents the service from hanging indefinitely if the cache is slow or unresponsive. A system might be configured to time out after 200 ms for each request to the cache.

Circuit breakers

A circuit breaker prevents further attempts to call a failing service after a certain number of failed attempts. If the cache continues to fail or is too slow, the circuit breaker "trips" and routes traffic to a fallback system (e.g., another cache or a database). The circuit breaker can automatically reset after a set period to test if the original service has recovered. For example, a circuit breaker might be configured to trip after five consecutive retries fail.

We'll start testing the checkout service by introducing small latencies to ensure the retry logic and timeout settings are functioning before scaling up to introduce more severe issues that will ultimately trigger the circuit breaker. If all goes well, we expect the system to fail over to an alternative data source. These are our steps.

Step 1: Conduct a simple latency experiment

We start with a test of our retry logic. We want to ensure the system is resilient if network issues arise, such as high latency or a temporary loss of connectivity. Our steady state is a responsive service that responds within an acceptable time limit.

Our hypothesis is that if the network experiences significant latency when trying to reach the cache, the system should use its retry logic and timeout settings to handle the issue gracefully, eventually tripping the circuit breaker to prevent further degradation of service.

We start small by injecting a small amount of network latency (e.g., 200 ms) between the checkout service and the cache.

We observe whether the retry logic kicks in and whether the service handles the delay within the acceptable time limit without user impact. We continue to monitor whether the system continues functioning as expected, pulling from the cache after the latency delay.

Step 2: Test resilience against a more significant network issue

Once we've tested our retry logic with a small latency, we can increase the scope and intensity of the experiment to simulate a more significant network issue. This tests our timeouts. We increase the network latency (e.g., from 500 ms to 1 second) to see how the service behaves under heavier load or network congestion. We test how the retry logic handles the extended delay. Does the service retry the call to the cache, and does it respect the timeout setting? If so, we increase the severity of the issue by causing the cache API to completely fail after a set number of retries.

Step 3: Validate that the circuit breaker fails over to an alternative

We next set experiment conditions to render the cache inaccessible. After retrying, the circuit breaker mechanism should be triggered. When the circuit breaker is tripped, the checkout service fails over to an alternative data source, such as another cache instance in a different data center (in this case, our Postgres database). While the Postgres database might be slower than the cache, the goal is to keep the service operational, albeit with slightly degraded performance.

AI agents can make this process even simpler by dynamically adjusting failure injection parameters using reinforcement learning. For example:

1. Start with 200 ms delays, then autonomously scale to 500 ms to 1 second based on real-time performance telemetry.

2. Limit experiment impact to 0.5% of transactions initially, expanding only after validating safety mechanisms.

3. Optimize trip thresholds (e.g., five failures to four) through historical success pattern analysis.

You can further scale the experiment to test the resilience of the failover by introducing similar network issues between the checkout service and the Postgres database to see how the system continues to adapt under increased failure conditions. By following this process, we gradually increase the complexity of the experiment to validate the system's resilience mechanisms, without jumping into major disruptions immediately.

It's important to note that the initial settings for resilience mechanisms are often based on educated guesses rather than precise data. This is another reason that testing through chaos engineering experiments is so crucial.

Injecting network latency is just one condition we can scale in a chaos experiment. We'll discuss other conditions later in this section.

Starting in Production-Like Environments

Another important best practice to minimize risk in chaos engineering is to test experiments in pre-production environments before moving to production. This allows us to experiment safely without impacting real users. We can rapidly iterate, adjust parameters, and observe results free from production constraints. Once we confirm system resilience in these settings, we promote our experiment to the next environment, eventually reaching production. Each promotion carries risk, so we proceed with caution. Configuration drift between environments can lead to discrepancies in experiment results. Maintaining the "start small and scale" approach when moving between environments is crucial in case we encounter issues. Thoroughly vetting our experiments in pre-production ensures that our experiments are well-designed and insightful without unintended consequences.

Leveraging Modern Tools

We looked extensively at an example of testing network latency in a chaos experiment. There are many other types of conditions that are important to test. Modern tools (such as Harness Chaos Engineering, Chaos Monkey, and LitmusChaos) can help here by offering extensive catalogs of predefined experiments. Modern tools will typically offer chaos engineering experiments across categories and common failure patterns, including:

Resource exhaustion

CPU exhaustion
Force high CPU utilization to simulate a process consuming excessive processing power.

Memory exhaustion
Consume all available memory to test how your application handles memory pressure and potential out-of-memory errors.

Disk I/O exhaustion
Generate heavy disk read/write operations to simulate storage bottlenecks.

Network bandwidth exhaustion
Saturate network bandwidth to test how your application performs under network congestion.

Network disruption

Network latency
Introduce delays in network communication between services or with external dependencies.

Packet loss
Simulate the loss of network packets to test how your application handles unreliable connections.

Network partition
Isolate parts of your network to simulate connectivity issues between services or availability zone outages.

DNS failures
> Simulate DNS resolution problems to test how your application handles DNS outages or incorrect responses.

Infrastructure failure

Node failure
> Terminate or shut down VMs or containers to simulate hardware failures.

Pod failure (Kubernetes)
> Kill or evict pods to test the self-healing capabilities of your Kubernetes deployments.

Availability zone outage
> Simulate the failure of an entire availability zone to test your disaster recovery plan and multiregion deployments.

Inference layer attacks
> Simulate GPU memory exhaustion during ML model serving.

Application-level faults

Service failure
> Stop or crash specific services within your application to test fault tolerance and service degradation.

Function failure
> Introduce errors or exceptions within specific functions or methods to test error handling and recovery mechanisms.

Data corruption
> Corrupt data in a database or storage system to test your data integrity and recovery processes.

State management

Time travel
> Manipulate the system clock to simulate time shifts, testing how your application handles time-sensitive operations or scheduled tasks.

State injection
> Inject specific data or states into your application to test its behavior under unusual conditions. Use GenAI to create plausible corrupt data entries matching schema constraints.

Dynamic scenario generation using AI

Architecture modeling
Use AI to analyze service dependencies (e.g., Redis cache → payment gateway → database) to create failure chains mirroring production environments.

Generative adversarial networks
Create novel failure modes by pitting AI models against each other to discover unexplored vulnerability combinations.

The more types of experiments we try, the more we can learn about weaknesses in our system and how we can strengthen our resiliency.

Newer tools can go beyond offering catalogs to analyze your system architecture to suggest targeted experiments that expose potential weaknesses specific to your setup. For example, for software built with a microservices architecture, a chaos engineering tool might analyze network traffic and dependencies to identify critical services and suggest experiments that target these specifically. A modern tool might also recommend injecting latency or errors into API calls between services to test resilience to communication disruptions.

For applications deployed with Kubernetes, the tool could analyze your Kubernetes deployments and suggest experiments that target specific pods, deployments, or namespaces to test replica scaling, resource limits, and health checks. Tools like Red Hat's Krkn use AI to profile Kubernetes pods to prioritize network-intensive services for partition tests. In the case of multiregion deployments, a modern tool might analyze your multiregion setup and suggest experiments that simulate regional failures or network partitions to test your disaster recovery plan and the ability of your application to failover to another region.

Learning from Others

Paying close attention to industry-wide incidents, particularly those affecting companies with similar tech stacks, is crucial for proactive risk mitigation. For instance, an OpenAI outage on December 11, 2024, serves as a stark reminder of how seemingly minor deployments can have cascading consequences.

In this case, a new telemetry service overwhelmed the company's Kubernetes control plane, triggering DNS failures that brought down its API, ChatGPT, and Sora platforms for hours. The impact was widespread and long-lasting: for several hours, developers and users couldn't access the services they rely on. Engineers identified the root cause within minutes but faced a major hurdle—without access to the Kubernetes control plane, rolling back or fixing the deployment was extremely challenging.

Let's look at a few targeted chaos engineering experiments to see how these cascading failures might have been prevented.

Experiment 1: Control plane overload simulation

First, we design an experiment to test our Kubernetes API server resilience. In this experiment, we would intentionally flood the Kubernetes API server with a high volume of read/write operations to mimic what the new telemetry service did in production. By running this test on a staging environment with a production-like scale, we could have spotted the exact threshold where the API server starts to fail. This early detection would inform better load limiting, improved alerting, and possibly a safer phased rollout strategy.

Experiment 2: DNS failure testing

This experiment would involve introducing latency or failures in the DNS resolution process—specifically targeting the components responsible for service discovery. Running this experiment helps confirm that essential services can continue functioning even if DNS is disrupted. We will discover if our caches, fallback mechanisms, or alternative routing strategies are sufficient. If not, we would know to invest in those areas before a real outage hits.

Example 3: Break-glass access drills

This last experiment (or drill) involves simulating a situation where engineers are locked out of the Kubernetes API under heavy load. By practicing emergency access methods—like having dedicated out-of-band channels or specialized tooling—teams can quickly revert or disable problematic deployments when the standard control plane is inaccessible. If this drill had been done beforehand, teams would have known exactly how to remove the faulty telemetry service within minutes, minimizing downtime.

Service-Level Objectives and Service Resiliency

We see how chaos engineering helps us uncover weaknesses and build more resilient systems. But how do we define "resilient"? How do we measure and track whether our systems are meeting our reliability goals? This is where SLOs and service-level indicators (SLIs) come in. Together, these provide the framework for defining and measuring the reliability of our services, giving us a clear target to aim for and a way to track our progress.

SLOs are the targets we set for the reliability of our services. SLIs are the specific metrics we use to measure whether we're meeting those targets. SLOs are typically expressed as a percentage of time or number of requests that must meet the defined SLI criteria. For example, *99.9% of requests should have a latency of under 200 milliseconds*. SLIs are the specific, measurable metrics that reflect the performance of your service from a user's perspective. They quantify aspects like availability, latency, error rate, throughput, and other relevant factors.

In essence, SLIs are *what* you measure, and SLOs are the *targets* you set for those measurements.

Establishing Reliability Targets

When establishing reliability targets, it's essential to align them with the overarching business needs. Monitoring and observability solutions provide many SLI metrics, but it is important to prioritize those that accurately reflect how your customers experience your applications. The goal is not to track every individual service, but to focus on those services that are critical to the customer experience.

Common SLIs include "the four golden signals":

Request latency
> The time taken to process a user request

Throughput
> The number of requests processed per second

Error rate
> The percentage of failed requests

Saturation
> The utilization percentage of the system

Consider carefully how to implement each of these within your system. For instance, when measuring latency (response time), you can choose to track all transactions or focus on a subset of the most crucial ones, such as login, payment submission, or adding items to a shopping cart. Again, select a metric that provides a meaningful representation of your customers' experience.

Shared Ownership of System Reliability

In Chapter 1, we introduced DevOps as practices that combine software development (Dev) and IT operations (Ops) concerns. Nowhere are shared ownership and collaboration more important than in ensuring system reliability. SLOs are a great example of this shared responsibility. Development, operations, and reliability teams should work together to define SLOs. The collaboration establishes an understanding of acceptable system performance and creates a common goal for everyone to work toward. SLOs then act as a guide for making decisions that balance the need for rapid development (velocity) with the need for stable and reliable systems.

With this shared understanding, developers can prioritize features that maintain reliability, knowing how their work impacts overall system performance. At the same time, operations teams gain the context they need to effectively support the application. If an SLO is breached, it triggers activities that encourage engineering teams to stabilize the service before releasing new features. This helps prevent a cycle of instability and ensures that reliability remains a top priority.

A collaborative approach to designing, prioritizing, and conducting the chaos engineering experiments themselves brings teams together. All teams benefit from the insights gained from these experiments and from working together to address when failures are found.

Modern tools facilitate this collaborative approach to system reliability. Monitoring platforms, incident management systems, and communication tools give a shared visibility into system performance and potential issues. Real-time data and automated alerts empower both Dev and Ops teams to respond quickly to incidents. More importantly, these tools foster a culture of proactive problem-solving (such as data-driven prioritization, real-time collaboration triage, etc.), where teams can identify and address potential issues before they impact users.

Error Budgets and Their Role in Reliability and Innovation

We've learned how chaos engineering helps us proactively find system weaknesses, and how SLOs and SLIs provide a clear framework for defining our reliability goals and measuring whether our systems are meeting those targets. Error budgets (*https://oreil.ly/K0JqJ*) enter to provide a safety net.

Error budgets represent the maximum amount of unreliability or downtime that a service can have while still meeting its SLOs. By tolerating minor hiccups in the pursuit of rapid innovation, error budgets acknowledge that perfection is unattainable, and instead help us achieve an acceptable level of reliability that balances these two competing priorities.

Let's look at how this works by returning to our e-commerce example. Imagine we've set an SLO of 99.9% for website logins taking less than 300 ms. Over a one-week period, this translates to a maximum allowable SLO violation time of 10.08 minutes. This is our error budget. How does that impact us? In the event that the error budget burns down to zero, we will stop or slow down deployments of new software and focus on stabilizing the system while our error budget replenishes. Not only does the state of our error budget impact our deployment priorities, but it also factors into chaos testing priorities.

Monitoring to Inform Chaos Testing Experiments

Keeping a close eye on your SLIs does more than just alert you to immediate problems—it reveals potential weaknesses in your system. For example, if you notice your system constantly pushing against latency limits, draining your error budget, your system might be struggling to keep up in high-traffic scenarios. This suggests a good area to focus your chaos experiments on. By simulating those high-traffic, high-latency situations, you can see how your system holds up under pressure and make sure it can still meet its SLOs during peak usage.

With modern tools, you can automate this by automatically triggering chaos tests based on these patterns, so you can continuously test and improve your system's resilience without lifting a finger. Modern platforms can correlate SLI trends with chaos test recommendations using AI, thus increasing test coverage significantly.

Strategic Use of Error Budgets for Chaos Testing Experiments

Error budgets are not merely a safety net for occasional failures; they are a tool for managing risk. Using our e-commerce website example, we think of the 10.08-minute error budget as a resource to be spent wisely. In this section we'll look at how to proactively use this budget to conduct chaos experiments.

Prioritizing chaos experiments in alignment with your available error budget

Effective chaos engineering requires consideration of your available error budget. When your error budget is healthy, your runway is long. You have more freedom to conduct aggressive experiments, simulating large-scale failures or pushing critical system components to their limits. This might involve testing failover mechanisms, injecting network latency, or even simulating the complete outage of a core service.

As your error budget dwindles, it's essential to shift focus toward smaller-scale experiments that carry less risk of significant disruption. These might involve testing individual components in isolation, simulating minor network issues, or validating the resilience of recent changes. Prioritizing experiments in this way ensures that you can continue to learn and improve without jeopardizing overall system stability.

Modern automation tools can help. By analyzing your error budget in real time, these tools can recommend appropriate experiments based on your available "room for failure." This allows you to maintain a balance between proactive testing and service reliability, ensuring that your chaos engineering efforts are both insightful and responsible.

Protect your error budget by utilizing AI-augmented dry runs and simulations

Simulating first is another strategy to minimize the risk of unintended consequences during chaos experiments. This is especially important when up against a dwindling error budget. The practice of AI-augmented "dry running" chaos experiments involves simulating experiments in a controlled environment, using system models or replicas, to assess their potential impact before executing them in production, and using AI remediation agents to roll back experiments if anomaly detection thresholds breach predefined limits. By identifying potential issues and refining experiment parameters beforehand, teams can reduce the likelihood of causing significant disruptions that could drain your error budget and cause significant disruptions.

Integrating Chaos Engineering and SLOs into CI/CD Pipelines

Reliability issues are primarily driven by change, changes to our applications, or changes to your infrastructure. Google DevOps Research and Assessment (DORA) defines the change failure rate (CFR) metric, which gives us another view of the challenge. The CFR describes how often our changes, such as new code deployments or infrastructure updates, introduce problems in production that require hotfixes or rollbacks. The DORA 2024 State of DevOps report indicates that 80% of surveyed teams have average CFRs of 20% of their releases. In fact, 25% of teams have CFRs averaging an alarming 40% of releases.

In addition, we must consider the time and cost to remediate each change failure. The failed deployment recovery time metric (replacing the similar mean time to recovery [MTTR] metric) focuses on how quickly an organization can recover from failures. This gives us a sense of the challenges teams face on this front. While many teams are able to remediate in less than a day, 25% require a week to a month to replace defective software.

Throughout earlier chapters, we've looked at strategies to prevent defects from getting to production. We test at every stage in our delivery pipelines, executing tests of every type. We take care in managing our environments. We guard against configuration drift with practices like GitOps, combined with IaC. And we conduct chaos engineering testing in pre-production and production environments to help us find weaknesses in our systems. Yet, despite our best efforts, occasional defects that require fast remediation are inevitable. This is where continuous resilience comes in.

Just as continuous integration and continuous delivery are about using automation to build, test, and deploy our code, continuous resilience is about automating our resiliency practices by adding chaos engineering experiments to our CI/CD pipelines. Doing so means we are not just testing functionality, but actively and constantly evaluating how changes stand to impact the stability of our systems. Using AI agents for DevOps, chaos experiments can be intelligently integrated into CI/CD pipelines.

In "Scaling Your Chaos Engineering Practices" we'll explore how to scale a chaos engineering practice by incorporating it into our delivery pipeline with the help of modern tools. We'll look at how to prioritize the experiments to add to your pipeline, and best practices for securing and governing chaos experiments in your pipeline.

Scaling Your Chaos Engineering Practices

Organizations start their chaos engineering journey in different ways. Often a single team or two will adopt an open source tool and introduce experiments in a small pocket of an organization. An organization may host periodic chaos engineering "game days." There are all-hands-on-deck, planned events where teams deliberately inject a series of failures into systems to practice incident response and identify weaknesses in a controlled environment. These are typically infrequent and responses are reactive to issues that are discovered.

The trick to implementing continuous resiliency at scale, across an organization, can be a matter of choosing the right tooling. While both open source and proprietary solutions offer valuable capabilities, organizations should carefully evaluate their requirements. Some enterprise environments may need specific features like advanced security controls, comprehensive audit trails, and RBAC—features that may vary in availability and maturity across open source solutions.

This challenge was acutely felt by a leading fintech company processing over a billion daily payment transactions. Faced with increasing transaction failures during peak demand, it sought a solution to improve the reliability of its complex platform supporting 20+ financial products.

The company's choice of a modern chaos engineering tool was instrumental in overcoming the obstacles of scaling its chaos engineering practices. The tool it chose (in this case, Harness Chaos Engineering) included an extensive library of prebuilt experiments that simplified the work of automating and orchestrating numerous chaos experiments. In addition, comprehensive analysis and reporting capabilities gave the company quick insights into the resiliency of its systems.

The company began by focusing on a single critical service that handled nine million daily payment requests. It pinpointed fault-tolerant targets within the intricate infrastructure, laying the groundwork for a controlled rollout of resilience testing. By prioritizing the automation of chaos experiments within delivery pipelines and production environments, it addressed the root causes of transaction failures and built a foundation for continuous resilience.

Through its automated resilience testing platform, the company was able to expand the breadth of its testing to uncover vulnerabilities in service recovery, optimize application design patterns, and fine-tune configurations. The results were significant: a 16× reduction in failed transactions, MTTR reduced to 10 minutes, and a 10× improvement in customer satisfaction. Without modern tooling that offers security, templates and automation, and orchestration, it would have been impossible to roll out chaos engineering across the organization and achieve these results in the short time it took.

Adding Chaos Engineering Experiments and SLOs to Your CI/CD Pipeline

To solidify your resilience strategy, integrate SLOs as reliability guardrails within your CI/CD pipeline. Think of SLOs as the brakes on a race car—essential for maintaining control while pushing for maximum speed. Development teams, much like race car drivers, strive for rapid deployments, but without robust SLOs in place, they risk crashing their systems with unchecked changes. By monitoring key metrics, you can automatically block deployments that breach these thresholds or exhaust their error budget. This approach can accelerate your development velocity without sacrificing stability.

When adding chaos engineering experiments to your CI/CD pipeline, keep in mind two measures to guide your progress: resilience scores and resilience coverage. Resilience scores are simply how well your services perform against the experiments you apply in QA and production. Resilience coverage, similar to code coverage, assesses how many more experiments are needed to comprehensively evaluate system resilience, guiding the creation of a practical number of tests. Together, these metrics provide a holistic view of resilience, enabling all teams to contribute to and measure progress toward continuous resilience goals.

Start by adding experiments that test against known resilience conditions, ensuring your resilience score remains stable with each new deployment. Slowly increase your resilience coverage by adding experiments to test new conditions. If increasing the resilience coverage means that the resilience scores are reduced, determine if the failed chaos experiment warrants stopping the pipeline or if action can be taken in parallel.

Next, add experiments that address changes to the platform on which the target deployments run. For example, when upgrading underlying platforms like Kubernetes, incorporate chaos experiments into your CI/CD pipeline to proactively identify potential weaknesses and compatibility issues. This helps prevent latent issues from impacting applications in the future and ensures a smooth transition during platform updates. By catching these issues early, you can avoid costly incidents and maintain continuous resilience.

Add experiments to the pipeline that validate the deployments against previous production incidents and alerts as incidents occur. Lastly, add experiments that validate the deployments against configuration changes to the target infrastructure. This is another scenario where the resilience tests that passed earlier will start failing because the target environment changed through a higher or lower configuration.

As you invest in creating and fine-tuning your experiments, treat them like any other piece of software: version them, test them, and manage their lifecycle in a repository. This ensures your chaos engineering practice remains effective and adapts to changes in your systems. Centralized repositories facilitate collaboration and the sharing of these experiments, promoting consistency and best practices across teams.

Security and Governance for Chaos Engineering

Clearly, chaos engineering is a powerful approach, but careless experimentation has the potential to cause serious harm to both system resilience and trust in your chaos engineering program. By integrating it with your security and governance frameworks, you can define the guardrails you need to ensure experiments are conducted responsibly.

Just like tech debt, resilience debt can accumulate in your production services. Every alert, incident, hotfix, or workaround—like simply throwing more resources at a problem—contributes to this debt. Instead of addressing the root cause, these quick fixes often mask underlying issues and create a false sense of stability.

Modern chaos engineering tools can help you establish and enforce policies to combat this. For example, we could set a policy that mandates a corresponding chaos experiment for every production incident related to component misbehavior, network issues, API failures, or unexpected load. This experiment, integrated into your CI/CD pipeline, would need to be validated within a specific timeframe, say, within 60 days of the incident. Such a policy would not only enforce a discipline of addressing resilience debt but also encourage developers and QA teams to prioritize fixing production code over pushing new features that might further exacerbate the problem.

In addition to using policies to manage resilience debt, you can use security governance policies to prevent unauthorized experiments, restrict access to critical systems, and limit testing by environment, time window, personnel, or even fault type. By automating oversight and integrating these policies into your CI/CD pipelines, you can increase resilience coverage while reducing risk.

The Future of AI-Native Chaos Engineering in Service Reliability

The future of chaos engineering promises even greater sophistication and integration within service reliability practices. Tools such as Harness Chaos Engineering and Chaos Monkey will not only automate experiments but also leverage AI/ML to predict their impact, analyze system behavior under stress, and recommend optimal mitigation strategies. This intelligent automation will minimize risk, allowing teams to conduct more complex experiments with greater confidence and efficiency. Advancements in observability and tracing will provide deeper insights into system dynamics, enabling more precise identification of vulnerabilities and faster recovery from disruptions.

As systems grow increasingly complex, with distributed architectures and microservices becoming ever-present, chaos engineering will play a crucial role in ensuring their resilience. Even large language model–based multiagentic systems can be enhanced using chaos engineering (*https://oreil.ly/g7tjd*). By combining chaos testing with AI-powered analysis and automated remediation (for example, ChaosEater (*https://oreil.ly/IKlJW*)), we will be able to address potential failures faster and with greater precision, minimizing downtime and maintaining high levels of service reliability.

Summary

In this chapter, we explored chaos engineering as a methodical approach to building and validating system resilience. We learned to design and execute experiments responsibly, using SLOs and error budgets to balance innovation and stability. By integrating chaos engineering into CI/CD pipelines and leveraging modern tooling, organizations can proactively identify weaknesses, learn from failures, and continuously improve resilience. Ultimately, chaos engineering empowers us to create more robust systems that meet the demands of today's complex digital world. With these principles in place, the next step is to apply them seamlessly as part of your deployment process. Let's explore how to ensure stability during production rollouts.

CHAPTER 7

Deploying to Production

The Knight Capital incident (*https://oreil.ly/pTAIv*) of August 1, 2012, stands as a stark example of how a software deployment gone wrong can have catastrophic consequences. On that day, Knight Capital, then one of the largest trading firms in the US, deployed a large update to its automated trading system. Due to a confluence of factors, including limited automation, human error in deployments, and poor feature flag management, outdated code was accidentally reactivated, causing the system to rapidly place erroneous orders in the stock market (*https://oreil.ly/efPYb*).

Within just 45 minutes, the faulty algorithm had executed over 4 million trades, resulting in a staggering loss of $460 million for the firm. This incident not only nearly bankrupted Knight Capital, leading to its eventual acquisition, but also caused significant market disruption. It highlighted the critical importance of robust deployment practices, thorough testing, governance, and fail-safe mechanisms in high-stakes software environments.

Deploying to production can be a high-stakes activity. While not every application is a market-making trading platform, applications worth updating have people who depend on them, and changing anything introduces risk. Although we might prefer to avoid this risk by deploying less often, we face business demands for more frequent change. Moreover, certain types of risk increase as we delay and accumulate more and more changes into our planned release, making the continuous delivery approach more valuable.

In previous chapters, as we've navigated the software delivery process, we've hit upon strategies to mitigate the risk of finally deploying to production. In Chapter 2, we discussed the importance of code reviews. In Chapter 3, we looked at how to use early scans and unit testing to detect issues quickly. Chapter 4 described additional types of testing to harden your software and reviewed best practices in deploying to test environments. By using consistent tooling, pipeline steps, and deployment strategies, and by parameterizing for differences in environments, we use our deployments to test environments to vet our deployments to production. In Chapter 5, we dived deep into security, reviewing the practices that help secure our production deployments.

Today, artificial intelligence is transforming how organizations approach production deployments to prevent such disasters. ML systems now analyze deployment patterns, detect anomalies during rollouts, and verify application health with greater precision than traditional monitoring. Unlike rule-based verification, which relies on predefined thresholds, AI systems can learn normal behavior patterns unique to each application and detect subtle deviations that might indicate emerging problems. These capabilities allow teams to deploy faster while paradoxically reducing risk—the opposite of the traditional speed-versus-safety trade-off.

In this chapter, in addition to covering the transformative role of AI, we'll look at best practices for governing production deployments and strategies to safely deploy to production, and we'll discuss observability to validate the quality of production deployments. We'll explore how modern AI-powered deployment tooling helps mitigate risk through intelligent verification rather than just reactive monitoring, and how AI-powered systems evaluate multiple signals simultaneously to determine deployment health, catching issues that might slip past human operators.

Governing Production Deployments

The Knight Capital incident is a good reminder: the consequences of deploying software with defects can be nothing short of catastrophic financial ruin. Your organization's trust and credibility are also at risk. For the organization, the cost of fixing defects post-deployment can skyrocket, far exceeding the expense of addressing them during development.

To deploy with confidence, we need to understand what code changed and who made those changes. We need to validate that the code review processes we put in place were conducted, and understand who conducted those reviews. For any dependencies that were introduced, we want to understand them and know that they comply with our policies. We want to know if they were reviewed for any known defects. We need assurance that the builds, scans, and test processes that we require were executed against all code changes. And of course, we want to ensure that the results of the scans and tests, in fact, met our criteria for passing. Lastly, we require evidence that our development processes themselves remain in compliance with the frameworks and requirements relevant to our organization.

Stringent code reviews, thorough and robust testing practices, and automated, repeatable deployment procedures are essential to avoiding deployment failures. However, without appropriate governance and controls to ensure that we've adhered to our processes, all of our efforts can be rendered ineffective.

AI is beginning to transform deployment governance, though most applications are still emerging. Current AI systems focus primarily on analyzing deployment patterns to identify risk factors and policy violations rather than making autonomous decisions. These systems can process more deployment variables simultaneously than humans, helping to identify subtle correlations between code changes, deployment configurations, and historical incidents. Organizations are beginning to use these insights to refine their governance frameworks, though human oversight remains essential for final approval decisions.

> Deployment governance is simply the systematic oversight and control of the software deployment process to ensure the rules and policies we've defined are enforced. Fundamentally, governance is about reducing the risk of change. Governance includes the policies, processes, and tools that organizations use to ensure that software deployments are carried out in a consistent, controlled, secure, and compliant manner. The challenge in governance is balancing the need for agility and innovation with the need for stability and risk management.

In the next few sections, we'll discuss traditional and modern approaches to deployment governance. We'll investigate how to automate the enforcement of our governing policies to make our delivery process more efficient. We'll review tools and strategies that support our governance processes, and lastly, we'll look at the future of deployment governance.

Traditional Approaches to Deployment Governance

Traditional approaches to deployment governance are those built for a pre-DevOps world. In this world, changes to production were infrequent, risky, and executed by a traditional operations team. Decision making was centralized and involved rigid processes.

The Information Technology Infrastructure Library (ITIL) is one widely adopted framework that characterizes a traditional approach. ITIL originally emerged in the 1980s as a response to the need for standardized IT management practices, evolving from a collection of best practices into a comprehensive framework. It includes several processes and practices that are directly relevant to deployment governance.

One of these is the change management process, which defines a structured approach for managing all changes to services and infrastructure, including deployments. It prescribes formal documentation of a proposed change, including its purpose, scope, impact, and risk assessment. A Change Advisory Board (CAB) or a similar body assesses changes. The change request is formally authorized or denied based on its merits and potential risks. If the change is approved and executed, a post-implementation assessment is conducted to ensure the change achieved its objectives and identify any lessons learned.

The release management process is similarly formal and orders the planning, scheduling, and controlling of releases into production environments. It's closely related to the change management process and is intended to ensure that deployments are executed in a controlled and transparent manner.

CABs are a typical feature of approaches like those defined by ITIL. A CAB is a committee of individuals responsible for formally assessing and approving or rejecting proposed changes to software. This board might include a change manager responsible for coordinating change request reviews and tracking change implementation, as well as technical experts, business stakeholders, security specialists, compliance officers, and others. The intention is to reduce risk through thorough evaluation of requests from several perspectives.

Moreover, CABs ensure accountability if anything does go wrong. While a highly functioning CAB will provide the intended oversight, at their worst CABs consist of inattentive reviewers that rubber-stamp reviews with little to no assessment. Or a CAB may be nominally effective but hopelessly inefficient. Email-driven approval processes are slowed by ignored emails, approvers being out of the office with no delegation, and review meetings getting rescheduled.

Research shows that these traditional CAB processes aren't just inefficient, they're actually counterproductive to the stability they aim to ensure. Writing about their landmark study of high-performing organizations in their book *Accelerate*, Forsgren, Humble, and Kim explain that "external approvals were negatively correlated with lead time, deployment frequency, and restore time and had no correlation with change fail rate." In other words, approval by external bodies like CABs demonstrably slows down delivery without improving stability.

This occurs because CABs divorce responsibility from knowledge; the people with the deepest understanding of the changes aren't the ones making approval decisions. While these committees create the appearance of due diligence, they often function as compliance theater, giving organizations someone to point to when things go wrong rather than actually preventing failures. The illusion of control they provide can even reduce vigilance among those implementing changes, since "the CAB approved it" becomes a shield against accountability.

The expense of CAB meetings, coupled with the ineffectiveness and delay, was tolerable when applications were released infrequently. As release frequencies have increased, the trouble with CABs is increasingly clear.

Modern Approaches to Deployment Governance

In previous chapters, we explored how to streamline the development process by automating steps at every stage, enabling faster and more frequent software releases. Modern approaches to deployment governance are similarly focused on automating the manual steps that are an unnecessary obstacle to releasing software.

Instead of relying on committees and manual approvals for deployment decisions, modern approaches favor automated decision making and deployments. Because the stakes of production deployment are so high, this must be done with great care. In this section we'll explore how.

In addition to automation, modern governance approaches also leverage contemporary strategies and tools to manage compliance. We'll look at how to use audit logs to simplify compliance, and tools like Open Policy Agent (OPA) to enforce security and regulatory standards.

Automating decision making

With modern CI/CD tools we can empower our pipelines to make autonomous deployment decisions. If we can ensure that our pipelines can adequately enforce governance policies to maintain our standards, we can accelerate software delivery by removing or minimizing manual approvals.

Consider these steps to automate deployment decision making in your delivery process:

1. Identify your "pass" criteria

Identifying clear criteria for promoting builds is crucial for automating your deployment process, but this can be challenging. One bank that we worked with documented its controls in a three-inch-thick binder containing hundreds of pages of regulations and policy. Often, decision makers may rely on both objective data and subjective judgment. Ambiguity can make it challenging to translate human decision making into a set of rigid, automated rules. For example, a decision maker might promote a build with a few minor test failures if they believe the issues are low risk and unlikely to impact users. However, translating this intuition into an automated rule that accurately assesses risk and user impact can be complex. AI has a growing role in bringing the fuzzier elements of human decision making into fully or mostly automated flows. If used this way, it should be required to explain its recommendations and insights.

2. Use "quality gates" to implement complex criteria to automate as many controls as possible

Gates are checkpoints within a CI/CD pipeline that evaluate specific criteria to determine whether a build should proceed to the next stage. Gates can take into account test results, code quality metrics based on static analysis results, code coverage, and adherence to coding standards, security scans results, and performance metrics. Other tools allow you to introduce a pipeline step that fails if the decision is "no," or you can set up conditional execution based on your specific criteria. Often, the simplest approach is to configure each set of tests to fail if it doesn't meet your standards. This way, if any step fails, the entire pipeline halts, preventing the promotion of a substandard build.

3. Consider historical results when automating nuanced decisions

For instance, security initiatives often start with a zero-tolerance policy for new high-priority issues but tolerate existing ones while the team works through them. This requires considering historical data, not just the most recent results.

4. Finally, standardize on that automation

Use the choice of standardization or painful manual compliance as an incentive to use standardized tooling. Teams at the bank that we worked with were given a choice to deploy to production by certifying that a release complies with all of the controls detailed in the binder, or by using their standardized automated processes and tooling. This became an easy choice.

Building strong audit trails to automate compliance

Deployment governance and compliance are closely related. Effective governance practices are crucial in achieving and maintaining compliance with various regulatory standards and frameworks.

We reviewed several frameworks in Chapter 5, specifically security-related ones. PCI DSS is one widely applicable example. It's used to ensure that all companies that accept, process, store, or transmit credit card information maintain a secure environment. Regardless of the size or number of transactions you process, if your organization handles cardholder data then you are subject to its requirements. The major card brands (Visa, Mastercard, etc.) may impose fines or restrict your ability to process card payments if compliance cannot be demonstrated.

While PCI DSS primarily focuses on securing cardholder data, several requirements directly pertain to the software development and deployment process. This is to ensure the overall security of the environment where this data is handled. For example, PCI DSS requires that you develop and maintain secure systems and applications by taking steps such as conducting reviews of custom code prior to release to production and addressing common coding vulnerabilities. PCI DSS also includes testing requirements, mandating internal and external penetration testing after any significant infrastructure or application upgrade or modification.

A strong and comprehensive audit trail is essential to demonstrating the practices that compliance requires. And while your organization may not be subject to PCI DSS requirements, many other frameworks that may be relevant will have similar requirements of your development and deployment processes.

Your source control and CI/CD systems play a vital role here by capturing the granular details of every action taken within the delivery pipeline, from code commits and builds to test results, deployments, and environment configurations, along with the associated user, timestamp, and any relevant metadata. This includes logging user actions, system events, artifact tracking, configuration changes, and external integrations. By storing this information in a structured and accessible format, CI/CD tools provide a versatile audit trail that is adaptable to any number of security and regulatory frameworks.

Tools that support a strong audit trail allow your organization to demonstrate compliance without maintaining separate logs for each framework. It also enables you to proactively address potential security or compliance concerns.

Managing enforcement with Policy as Code

Policy as Code (PaC) can be instrumental in automating your production deployments while maintaining robust governance. PaC is the practice of defining and managing security, compliance, and operational policies *as code*, allowing for automated enforcement. Policies are defined in a declarative language and can be managed like any other critical piece of code: versioned in source control, allowing for tracking, collaboration and required code reviews, and rollback capabilities.

OPA is a popular open source policy engine used to implement PaC. With OPA, every deployment is automatically evaluated against your defined policies, ensuring consistent enforcement without slowing down your delivery process. Imagine your deployment policy requires all container images to be scanned for critical vulnerabilities before reaching production. Using OPA, you can express this PaC, and integrate it into your pipeline. Now, every time a deployment is triggered, OPA automatically scans the image and either allows the deployment to proceed if the image is clean or halts it if vulnerabilities are found. This eliminates manual security checks and ensures consistent adherence to your security standards without human intervention.

OPA's versatility extends beyond security checks. You can codify various deployment policies, such as enforcing canary deployments, requiring approvals for specific changes, or validating resource configurations. By automating these checks, you gain confidence that every deployment adheres to your organization's standards and regulatory requirements. This not only accelerates your delivery process but also reduces the risk of human error and noncompliance.

Safeguarding the Deployment Process

Tightly controlling your governance mechanisms helps protect your deployment. Developer empowerment is also critical in modern deployments. In practice, you need to strike a balance between the two. While you want to enable developers to adapt their deployment pipelines, you also need to safeguard against potential risks. Malicious actors can tamper with or bypass the very governance mechanisms you put in place, or they can be corrupted by human error. Alternatively, overly tight controls on deployments can create another obstacle to efficient deployments.

OPA can help here too. With OPA you apply strict controls on the policy update process itself, ensuring that any changes to your governance framework are carefully vetted and compliant. By centralizing policy rules in OPA and applying them to pipelines, you create a separation of concerns. This makes it more difficult for individual developers to circumvent policies, as they would need to modify the central OPA policies, which can be subject to stricter access controls, peer reviews, and audit trails.

As we increasingly rely on AI to generate our pipelines for us, OPA policies provide both directional input to the AI as to what we want, and protection ensuring that the output of the AI is in compliance with our standards.

Another important control in safeguarding your deployment process is implementing robust RBAC. As discussed in Chapter 2, RBAC allows you to granularly control who has access to modify pipelines and sensitive configuration settings within your CI/CD platform. This ensures that only authorized personnel can make changes to your deployment process, minimizing the risk of malicious activities.

By combining these approaches, you can centralize policy enforcement, ensuring your deployments are tamper-proof and effectively monitored.

Future Trends in Deployment Governance

As in nearly every area of software development, AI and ML will drive important future trends in deployment governance. Predictive analytics, for example, is a branch of data analytics that applies ML techniques for analyzing historical data to predict future outcomes. Applied to software deployments, predictive analytics can be used to identify patterns and risk factors to flag potential issues. Vendors are creating dashboards, such as Digital.ai's "Change Risk Prediction," based on trends like team failure rates and defects found in testing. Today, most of these solutions are relatively straightforward correlations found in broad sets. It's not unreasonable to expect more insights from models as we go forward, especially from DevOps platforms with easy access to wider data sets.

Your team can proactively address problems before they impact users. AI and ML can be used to automatically enforce governance policies in real time, analyzing code changes, configurations, and deployments to ensure compliance with security and operational standards. These advancements will empower organizations to deliver software with increased speed, confidence, and resilience.

Reconciling Traditional and Modern Approaches

Within a traditional governance approach, ITIL defines a standard change as a pre-approved, low-risk change with a well-defined procedure, allowing for quicker implementation with minimal formal authorization. By using modern DevOps practices, relying on quality gates and modern policy enforcement, we can significantly de-risk even complex software deployments. This level of control and reliability allows these deployments to be treated as standard changes. Essentially, the inherent risk mitigation within modern DevOps practices aligns with ITIL's goal of standardized, predictable change management, enabling faster and more frequent deployments without compromising stability or compliance.

In "Production Deployment Strategies" we'll explore using progressive deployments to further de-risk production deployments.

Production Deployment Strategies

In Chapter 4 we covered how to automate our deployment processes, and we have now looked at how to mitigate risk through deployment governance practices. Next we turn our attention to the actual business of deploying our software to production. In this section we'll look at how to further mitigate risk with progressive deployment techniques. With even the strongest governance and the most cautious progressive deployments, our deployments may still fail. We must come prepared with a rollback strategy, so we'll look at approaches to revert quickly. Lastly, we'll look at tool selection. Choosing modern tools can help you make governance, progressive deployments, and rolling back easy.

The Traditional Big-Bang Deployment

Before we look at modern approaches, we can remind ourselves of the traditional approach—and what still may be required for some elements of stateful applications. Traditionally, we would take our application offline, upgrade every instance of every component of the application, and start the application back up. After a quick validation, we would expose it back to users, and watch it for a period of time to make sure it looked healthy before deeming the deployment a success. If there was a problem, we would take the application back offline and roll back the application to the best of our ability—often a daunting challenge.

This traditional approach required application downtime, introduced significant risk, and demanded significant attention from engineers. The opportunities to do better are abundant.

Using a Progressive Delivery Strategy

Software deployments can be like walking a tightrope—one wrong step and the consequences can be severe. But progressive deployment strategies offer you a safety net. By gradually rolling out changes and closely monitoring their impact, these strategies minimize risks and allow for quick course correction if problems arise. In this section we'll look at a number of popular deployment strategies including rolling updates, blue-green deployments, canary deployments, and the use of feature flags.

Deploying rolling updates

Rolling deployments are a very common delivery strategy in which you gradually update an application or service by incrementally replacing instances of the old version with the new version. This is done in a controlled manner, ensuring that a certain number of instances are always available to handle user traffic during the update process.

Rolling deployments have distinct advantages. They minimize downtime as the application remains accessible throughout the update process. Importantly, rolling deployments reduce risk. By updating instances incrementally, potential issues with the new version can be detected and addressed early on, limiting their impact. And this type of deployment can be customized to fit specific application needs, allowing for endless adjustments to the speed and scale of the update process.

However, implementing and managing rolling deployments can be more complex than other deployment strategies, especially for large-scale or distributed systems. There is also potential for inconsistencies. During the update process, two different versions of the application, running simultaneously, could lead to differences in data or user experience. In addition, rolling back an ongoing deployment can be complicated, and additional steps to preserve data integrity are required.

Implementation options are numerous. Kubernetes provides built-in support for rolling updates through its Deployment object. New pods with the updated version are gradually created, and old pods are terminated once the new ones are ready. Container orchestration platforms (e.g., Docker Swarm, Nomad) offer similar mechanisms for rolling updates, allowing for incremental replacement of containers or services. Load balancers can be used to implement rolling updates by gradually shifting traffic from old instances to new instances as they become available. In some cases, rolling deployments might be implemented using custom scripts or automation tools that manage the update process and monitor the health of the application.

While rolling deployments require effort to implement, they offer a valuable option for minimizing downtime and risk during application updates.

Using blue-green deployments

A blue-green deployment is a release strategy that involves maintaining two identical environments, typically referred to as "blue" and "green." At any given time, only one of these environments (usually blue) is live, serving production traffic.

When a new version of your application is ready, it is deployed to the inactive environment (green). After testing and verification in the green environment, traffic is switched over from the blue environment to the green environment, making the new version live. Where a rolling deployment makes updates over time and different traffic will experience different versions of the service, a blue-green typically features a hard cutover. A switch is flipped and traffic, or at least new traffic, is moved immediately from the old to the new. Figure 7-1 depicts blue and green environments before and after deploying an update.

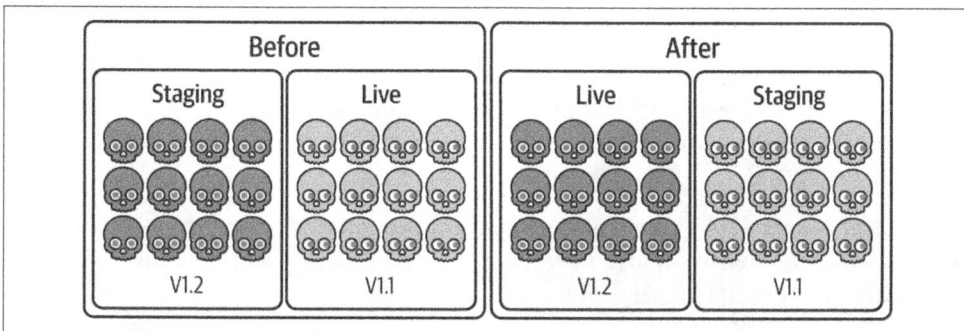

Figure 7-1. Blue-green deployments involve running two identical environments for seamless updates and rollback options (in the print book, blue appears in dark gray and green appears in light gray)

The previous live environment (now blue) can be used for the next deployment, kept as a backup in case a rollback is needed, or decommissioned.

A blue-green strategy offers distinct advantages:

Reduced downtime
  Traffic is switched between environments, minimizing any disruption to users and reducing downtime.

Easy rollbacks
  If there are issues with the new deployment, traffic can be quickly switched back to the previous version.

Improved testing
  The new version can be tested in a production-like environment before going live.

The main disadvantage lies in the increased infrastructure cost, as maintaining two separate, identical environments can be expensive. Additionally, blue-green deployments might not be suitable for applications with complex state management or database schema changes, because synchronizing data between environments can be challenging.

A more advanced blue-green model can overcome most of the infrastructure cost challenge by integrating IaCM practices. During steady-state production, only one instance is in existence. At the start of the deployment, the deployment triggers an IaCM tool to provision a new instance, so both blue and green exist. At the conclusion of the process, the excess instance is de-provisioned. As a result, the excess infrastructure only needs to exist for the duration of the blue-green deployment.

Using canary releases

Canary releases offer another progressive strategy similar to rolling updates. A new version of the application is rolled out to a small subset of users or servers. This "canary" group acts as a test bed, allowing you to monitor the new version's performance and stability in a real-world production environment before making it available to all users.

In a typical canary deployment, only a small portion of traffic (e.g., 5% to 10%) might be directed to the newly deployed version. The performance, stability, and error rates of the new version are closely monitored and compared with those of the existing version. Metrics like response times, CPU usage, and error logs are analyzed to identify any potential issues. If the new version performs well in the canary environment, the percentage of traffic directed to it is gradually increased, allowing more users to access it. This process continues until the new version completely replaces the old one. If any issues or performance degradation are detected during the canary phase, the deployment can be rolled back quickly, minimizing the impact on users.

Canary deployments may be implemented with simple metric thresholds, but they increasingly leverage AI or ML capabilities to determine whether the new version performs satisfactorily. Traditionally, canary deployments have focused on performance benchmarks, but we can expect that in the future they will increasingly also tap into business metrics, stopping the rollout if the new version of the application is harming the business, even if it is not crashing.

While both canary deployments and rolling updates aim for gradual and controlled software releases, they differ in their focus. Rolling updates solve for minimizing downtime and service disruption across a service infrastructure. Canary deployments focus on metric-guided decision making about whether to gradually increase traffic to a new release or roll back to the previous version.

Using feature flags

Feature flags provide a strategy for deploying *features* in a progressive manner. Think of feature flags like hidden switches within your code, allowing you to turn features on or off for specific users or groups without deploying new code. This gives you granular control over who sees what, enabling A/B testing and targeted rollouts. Feature flags are similar to other progressive deployment strategies in that they allow you to monitor performance and gather feedback in a real-world environment and use this information to mitigate risks. However, feature flags operate at different levels; they control functionality within a single version. Other progressive strategies test an entirely new version.

Feature flags offer benefits beyond deployment risk mitigation, and we'll return to them in Chapter 8.

Rolling back

We've explored a few progressive deployment strategies, but your options are innumerable. Variations and hybrid approaches that blend elements of rolling updates, blue-green deployments, canary releases, and feature flags are all possibilities. The common thread among these strategies is a controlled rollout, allowing you to stop a deployment and roll back to a previous version if you need to. With a strategy like blue-green deployments, this is an easy proposition: your previous version stands at the ready. With a rolling update or a canary deployment, the rollback process is a matter of removing traffic from nodes with the defective software and then systematically replacing those nodes with the previous software version.

Rolling back involves not only redeploying the previous stable version of software, but also its associated configurations, dependencies, and data. Rolling back to a previous state can be as complex or more complex than the deployment itself. Certain deployment approaches will facilitate dependable rollbacks. For example, if the deployment is idempotent, meaning it can be repeated and achieve the same, nondestructive results, a redeploy of a prior version will be equivalent to a rollback.

Testing rollbacks is crucial to ensuring you can roll back without fear. It's not enough to simply have a rollback mechanism in place; you need to regularly validate its readiness. This involves simulating various failure scenarios and then executing the rollback procedure to ensure it swiftly and reliably restores the previous stable version. Thorough rollback testing verifies that the application, its data, and its dependencies are correctly reverted. Depending on the application and its data storage mechanisms, rollbacks may require data restoration or migration to ensure data consistency. Regularly test procedures to ensure they work as expected in all scenarios.

With complete confidence in your rollback procedures, you can then configure rollbacks to trigger automatically based on deployment health. Verifying deployment health is a topic we'll get into in the next section. Instead of relying on manual intervention, the system automatically reverts to the previous stable version when predefined thresholds are breached. This not only reduces the burden on your operations team but also takes human error out of the equation to minimize downtime.

Special considerations for specific architectures

Deployment and rollback complexities vary significantly depending on the software architecture. Monoliths, with their tightly coupled codebase, often require complete deployments and rollbacks that impact the entire system. Microservices, on the other hand, offer more granular deployments and rollbacks, targeting individual services. However, this interconnectedness means that dependencies must be carefully managed to ensure consistency across services. Distributed monoliths share characteristics of both monolithic architecture and microservices and combine the deployment complexities of microservices with the interdependency issues of monoliths.

Databases add another layer of complexity. When updates involve breaking changes to the structure of persistent data, strategies like "expand and contract" are needed. This strategy involves adding new database fields or tables alongside the existing ones, deploying the updated application to utilize the new structure, and eventually phasing out the old fields. The approach is complex to implement, but it is often required to ensure data integrity when supporting progressive deployment strategies and clean rollbacks.

Choosing the Right Tools

Armed with a progressive deployment strategy and robust rollback capabilities, you can deploy to production with confidence. But to truly unlock the power of these strategies, you need the right tools at your disposal. Modern deployment tools make all the difference, offering seamless support for progressive deployment strategies out of the box.

When selecting a tool to orchestrate your software deployments, it's essential to look beyond the basics and consider how well a given tool aligns with your specific needs. If you're planning a transition to automated deployment decisions alongside adopting new continuous delivery tools, understanding all the factors that go into your promotion decisions up front will help you choose the right tool with the required governance and gate capabilities. In addition, ensure that the deployment tool seamlessly integrates with your target environments, whether it's the cloud, on-premise servers, or a hybrid setup. Equally important is the tool's ability to handle your specific application types and architectures, including any complex database deployments or coordinated multiservice releases.

Beyond infrastructure and architecture compatibility, the deployment tool should include out-of-the-box support for your preferred progressive deployment strategies, ensuring you can easily implement canary releases, rolling updates, or other techniques. Robust rollback mechanisms should be a first-class concern, because they allow you to quickly revert to a previous stable version in case of unexpected issues. Furthermore, consider whether the tool integrates with your existing feature flag management system or offers its own feature flagging capabilities, giving you granular control over feature releases.

Verifying Production Deployments

Even the most diligent governance doesn't eliminate the need for robust practices to systematically verify your production deployments. In this section we'll look at the role of observability. We'll discuss modernizing your verification processes and look at testing strategies specific to production deployment verifications.

Observability in Deployments

Verifying your deployment starts with observability. Observability (*https://oreil.ly/ 94AtC*) simply refers to the ability to understand a system's internal state by examining its external outputs. Observability gets you from knowing that something is wrong to understanding why it's wrong, which enables faster troubleshooting and more effective root cause analysis. Observability data encompasses three key pillars:

Metrics
> These provide quantitative measurements of system performance, such as response times, error rates, and resource utilization. By tracking trends and anomalies in these metrics, teams can quickly identify potential issues and assess the impact of a new deployment.

Logs
> Logs offer detailed records of events and errors occurring within the application and its infrastructure. Analyzing log data helps pinpoint the root cause of problems and understand the sequence of events leading to an issue.

Traces
> Traces provide a visual representation of how requests flow through the system, highlighting bottlenecks, latency issues, and dependencies between different services. This helps identify performance issues and optimize application architecture.

Modernizing the War Room

Traditional deployment verification often resembles a high-stakes war room scenario with engineers monitoring dashboards and logs, ready to manually intervene at the first sign of trouble. The process is highly manual, relying on human interpretation of observability data. It is also reactive, with teams often only scrambling to address issues after they have impacted users.

This approach is not only stressful and inefficient but also prone to misses and slow response times. Moreover, it often leads to inconsistent verification procedures and limited visibility into the root cause of issues.

Modernizing deployment verification involves automating these manual tasks and human decisions. Instead of relying on engineers to monitor dashboards and logs, automated systems take over, continuously analyzing telemetry data and triggering alerts when anomalies are detected. The shift from reactive to proactive monitoring reduces the need for human intervention and accelerates response times.

The trick to achieve this automation is to integrate your deployment tools with your observability platforms. The integration can take different forms depending on the tools used. In one approach, your CI/CD tool notifies the observability platform when a deployment is in progress, providing a "hook" that can be used to trigger a rollback. The observability platform then analyzes telemetry data and decides whether to initiate a rollback, calling the hook provided by the CD tool.

Alternatively, CD tools like Harness can be configured to watch one or more observability tools for signs of trouble during the deployment process. If issues are detected, the CD tool can automatically trigger its own rollback mechanism, halting the deployment and reverting to a previous stable version. This tight integration between deployment and observability tools enables a seamless and automated verification process, minimizing downtime and ensuring faster feedback loops.

In either case, the industry no longer tolerates outages and seeks to detect indicators that trouble is brewing before an application fails. As a result, AI/ML is used to analyze multiple data sources to identify anomalies that indicate a likelihood of failure. AI anomaly detection has become a central component in modern deployment verification. Unlike traditional monitoring, which relies on predefined thresholds, these systems build statistical models of normal application behavior across hundreds of metrics and can detect complex, multidimensional anomalies that would be impossible to define with static rules. This capability is particularly valuable during the critical minutes following a production deployment, when subtle performance issues might otherwise go unnoticed until they escalate into user-impacting incidents.

Deployment verification systems integrate these AI capabilities into automated verification gates, providing continuous assessment throughout the deployment process rather than point-in-time checks. When anomalies are detected, these systems can automatically pause progressive rollouts, or even automatically trigger the rollback process.

Testing Production Deployments

We discussed testing at length in Chapter 4. We return now to look at test strategies particularly suited to verifying in production. Verifying production deployments requires a layered testing approach.

Synthetic testing can be paired with phased or progressive deployments. By simulating typical user interactions and transactions in a production environment, synthetic tests run through scenarios to catch issues quickly. This allows teams to address problems early on, either by rolling back the deployment or by implementing necessary fixes.

Beyond the initial deployment phase, ongoing testing in production is essential for ensuring long-term stability and performance. Synthetic testing continues to play a valuable role, providing continuous monitoring of critical user journeys and identifying any regressions or performance degradations. Chaos engineering, which we covered in Chapter 6, takes this a step further by deliberately injecting failures into the system to test its resilience and ability to recover.

Another important aspect of ongoing testing is progressive feature disclosure. This involves gradually rolling out new features to a subset of users, allowing teams to gather feedback and monitor performance before a full release. Techniques like A/B testing enable comparisons between different versions of a feature, helping identify the most effective implementation. This controlled approach to feature releases minimizes risk and allows for data-driven decisions based on real user behavior. By combining synthetic testing, chaos engineering, and progressive feature disclosure, organizations can establish a comprehensive testing strategy that ensures continuous verification and improvement of their production deployments.

Summary

As AI continues to transform production deployments, the connection between deployment strategies and feature management becomes increasingly important. AI-powered deployment verification systems don't just monitor overall application health; they can now track the impact of individual features within a deployment, providing granular insights that inform both rollback decisions and future feature releases. These systems create a continuous feedback loop where deployment data feeds into feature flag decisions, and feature behavior informs deployment strategies. Modern platforms analyze feature performance patterns across deployments to recommend which features should be gradually released through feature flags versus those that can be safely deployed traditionally. This intelligence helps teams balance development velocity with operational stability, creating a more sophisticated approach to managing both deployments and features in production environments. In Chapter 8, we will focus in depth on feature management.

CHAPTER 8

Feature Management and Experimentation

In Chapter 7, we explored the challenges and best practices for deploying software to production. We focused on strategies to mitigate risk and ensure reliability, looking at progressive deployment strategies, paired with robust rollback mechanisms. This approach helps us identify issues in new software versions early to safeguard the integrity of production systems. Recall that we touched on feature flags as one important progressive deployment strategy; feature flags are a mechanism to deploy individual features within a single version of software in a progressive way. In this chapter, we will continue the discussion on the use of feature flags as a tool for managing feature deployment.

We will also dive deep into another role of feature flags—how they can drive experimentation. While feature flags are great for reducing deployment risks and enabling progressive delivery, their impact goes far beyond that. When enhanced with AI, they empower you to run experiments to learn about your users, optimize your feature design ideas, validate hypotheses, and make data-driven decisions that improve product usability, engagement, and overall business outcomes.

Feature management and experimentation management are closely related—feature flags are the fundamental on/off switches that control whether a specific piece of functionality is enabled. Feature management systems provide the infrastructure for controlling how and when features are released to which users under which conditions, while experimentation leverages this control to measure the impact of each variation and help teams make data-driven decisions. However, as powerful as feature management with feature flags is, they come with their own risks and challenges, which we'll also explore.

Recall our discussion of the Knight Capital incident in Chapter 7. A faulty software deployment led to $460 million in losses within 45 minutes. The incident occurred when Knight Capital deployed a new version of its trading software that reactivated a dormant piece of legacy code. A misconfigured feature flag was to blame. This flag, meant to control whether a piece of legacy code was active or inactive, was mistakenly enabled on some servers but not others. The inconsistency triggered outdated logic, leading to over four million erroneous trades in less than an hour.

While feature flags offer immense potential to help teams deliver at scale, as the Knight incident shows, their misuse or mismanagement can introduce significant risks. Effective feature management requires thoughtful planning, thorough testing, and strong governance to prevent these kinds of disasters.

AI is transforming feature management systems by making experimentation and implementation dramatically more accessible and insightful. Modern AI-powered platforms can interpret statistical results in plain language, suggest optimal rollout strategies based on user patterns, automatically detect anomalies, and even generate implementation code tailored to specific experiments. AI augmentation reduces the cognitive load on developers while enabling product teams to perform more sophisticated experimentation.

In this chapter, we'll examine the limitations of traditional homegrown feature management solutions that lack AI capabilities, and explore how modern, AI-enhanced systems not only reduce risks but also unlock the full potential of feature management and experimentation as strategic tools for delivering high-quality software.

Benefits of Feature Management in Modern Software Development

Imagine that our organization is implementing a payment platform that handles basic online transactions for small businesses. This platform supports payment processing, invoicing, basic analytics, and integrations with e-commerce platforms. We release new features continuously and rapidly to make iterative improvements and address user feedback.

In this section, we'll look at how we can use modern feature management to free our organization from the constraints of traditional release processes in order to speed up our payment platform release cycles. We'll discuss how to use feature management to support collaboration across teams and progressive delivery. Lastly, we will look at how feature flags can help us manage technical debt.

Speeding Up Development Cycles with Feature Flags

At their simplest, feature flags let us deploy new features that are "turned off," decoupling deployment from feature release. Then, we can flip our feature flag like a switch to activate the feature later on, without having to deploy new code. This approach helps us realize trunk-based development. As we looked at in Chapter 2, continuous integration involves regularly merging code changes into a shared repository, with automated testing ensuring the quality of each integration. Trunk-based development builds on this by encouraging developers to make small, frequent commits directly to the main branch, often called the "trunk."

AI-powered systems speed the transition to trunk-based development by generating the code needed to wrap code blocks with feature flags from a simple prompt. This reduces the cognitive burden on developers who may be new to feature flagging. Wrapping all new changes with feature flags ensures the main branch remains stable, even with frequent small commits.

Alternatives to trunk-based development involve long-lived feature branches. With these alternatives, integration becomes increasingly difficult over time because when multiple teams work in isolated branches for extended periods, they often discover costly conflicts only during integration. The delayed integration also weakens the benefits of continuous integration practices, as problems might not be detected until long after the code was written. Trunk-based development is widely regarded as an industry best practice because it helps teams minimize merge conflicts and maintain a steady flow of updates to the main branch. The more frequently changes are merged, the higher the likelihood that the main branch remains deployable at any moment. This means faster, more reliable releases.

In the absence of feature flags, it's difficult to deploy the small changes that characterize trunk-based development because all changes become immediately active in the production environment. This necessitates tight synchronization of releases among teams, limiting the ability to safely merge and deploy incomplete features.

Feature flags provide an elegant solution to this challenge. By enabling developers to wrap new features or experimental changes within feature flags, they can commit their work to the main branch even if the functionality is not fully developed or is not production-tested. The flag effectively acts as a gatekeeper, ensuring that the incomplete feature remains turned off in production until you are ready. The approach eliminates the need for long-lived feature branches. This helps teams maintain a high deployment velocity and validate other aspects of the codebase without being hindered by feature completion timelines.

Decoupling Teams to Reduce Coordination Overhead

Going back to our payment platform, let's say we want to introduce a new "Subscription Payments" feature. The frontend team is responsible for updating the user interface to support recurring payment options, the backend team must implement APIs for managing subscription plans, and the analytics team is tasked with tracking user behavior for subscriptions.

Without feature flags, the release becomes a tightly coupled, high-risk event. The frontend team can't deploy the updated UI until the backend APIs are live, leaving their work unfinished in staging. The backend team can't fully test APIs because the frontend isn't integrated, delaying the validation of workflows. The analytics team can't implement tracking because the subscription system isn't functional in production.

This dependency forces all teams to align their schedules and coordinate a large, monolithic, and risky rollout. Any delays by one team ripple across the others, creating bottlenecks. If a critical bug is discovered, rolling back the feature means undoing work across all teams, often requiring a redeployment of the entire application.

Using feature flags, each team can work independently and release their changes incrementally. The frontend team can deploy the subscription management UI early, hiding it behind a feature flag. Doing so allows them to validate basic functionality in production while awaiting backend readiness. The backend team can implement and deploy subscription APIs to production, also gated by a feature flag. These APIs can be tested with test data or limited users, even if the frontend is not yet live. The analytics team can add tracking mechanisms and deploy them behind another flag. They can simulate user flows to ensure metrics are collected correctly without exposing the functionality to actual users.

Once all components are ready, the feature flags are toggled on for internal testing. Once validated internally, the feature can then be rolled out to production. Not only have we reduced the risk in releasing the "Subscription Payments" feature, but we've also reduced the overhead in coordinating across multiple teams. With AI-powered feature flags, this coordination becomes even more streamlined. AI assistants can automatically suggest flag dependencies across teams, alert when conflicts might arise, and even recommend optimal sequencing for multiteam feature releases based on historical deployment patterns.

Supporting Progressive Delivery with Phased Rollouts

When our "Subscription Payments" feature is ready to go, we can use feature flags to gradually roll out the update. With modern feature flag systems we can apply target criteria, such as user attributes or percentages, to enable a feature for a subset of users. This allows us to verify in production by slowly enabling the feature, monitoring its performance, and making adjustments before expanding to a larger audience.

During the phased rollout, we are looking at key metrics such as API error rates, response times, payment success rates, and customer feedback. If we observe anomalies, like a spike in failed payment attempts, increased latency, or reports of a broken user experience, they could indicate that the new feature has introduced issues that we need to investigate before proceeding.

AI significantly enhances progressive rollouts through predictive targeting and adaptive control. ML models analyze user behavior patterns and predict optimal rollout strategies—determining which users should see a feature first for maximum impact. During rollout, AI systems can monitor metrics in real time and automatically adjust the pace based on performance data, accelerating successful deployments while quickly identifying and containing problematic ones.

If we do find problems, we can easily roll back by simply toggling the flag off. The new functionality is disabled for all users without requiring a redeployment of the codebase. The system instantly reverts to the stable, previously tested version of the application, minimizing disruption and giving the team time to investigate and address the issue.

Manage Tech Debt with Feature Flags

Feature flags aren't just for launching new functionality—they can serve as a safety net when modernizing legacy code. In this way they act as a dimmer switch rather than just an on/off button. When refactoring, you can gradually transition from old code to new implementations while maintaining the ability to roll back if issues arise.

Modern, AI-native feature management systems excel at managing this complexity by tracking feature flag usage patterns and identifying flags that are no longer needed. ML algorithms can analyze code dependencies, flag states, and usage metrics to automatically identify obsolete flags and recommend their removal, preventing the accumulation of technical debt while maintaining system integrity.

Here's how this typically works in practice: First, you write your new, improved code implementation alongside the existing code. You then create a feature flag that lets you control which version runs—the old or new implementation. This allows you to test the new code in production with a small percentage of traffic while most users continue using the proven legacy code. As you gain confidence in the new implementation, you can gradually increase the percentage of traffic it handles.

This approach is particularly valuable for large-scale refactoring projects. Rather than performing a risky "big bang" replacement, you can use feature flags to migrate users in controlled waves. If you discover any issues, you can immediately revert to the old system for affected users without disrupting your entire user base.

The true power of this pattern emerges in complex systems where multiple components are being modernized simultaneously. Feature flags give you fine-grained control over your modernization effort, letting you coordinate multiple refactoring initiatives while maintaining system stability.

Optimizing Results Through Experimentation

We've seen how feature flags can help us release faster with trunk-based development and eliminate the need for coordinated multiteam rollouts. We've also seen how we can derisk our releases with progressive feature rollouts. But does this matter if we are not releasing features that provide value? This is where AI-powered experimentation comes in.

Only a handful of feature management systems include robust support for experimentation, enabling teams to run controlled, measurable tests directly within their existing application infrastructure. By combining fine-grained targeting, randomized percentage assignments for user populations, and automated statistical analysis, these systems allow engineering and product teams to conduct experiments seamlessly within the same infrastructure used for feature rollouts. This eliminates the need for separate experimentation platforms, which means you only need to manage, monitor, and write integration code for a single pattern.

Well-designed experiments transform product development. Rather than relying on subjective opinions and endless debates, you can use real-world user behavior to guide your decisions. Doing so replaces conference room speculation and endless debate with concrete data about the changes and new features that will actually engage your users. Feature flags allow us to segment users into groups (e.g., A and B) and expose each group to different variations of a feature. For example, in an online payment platform, one group might see a "Quick Pay" button, while another experiences an updated "Express Checkout" workflow.

By using feature flags, we can deploy these variations live in parallel, enabling side-by-side experiments that provide real-time, direct comparisons between versions. This approach offers a clear advantage over testing variations in succession, where differences in regular fluctuations, seasonal differences, the presence of marketing campaigns, or other factors can skew results. With side-by-side experiments, we ensure that both versions are subjected to the same conditions to get the most reliable and accurate insights. These comparisons help us confidently identify the version that delivers the most value to users, without the noise and uncertainty that come from sequential testing.

Modern AI dramatically accelerates our experimentation capabilities. For example, an ML approach known as the "multiarmed bandit" uses reinforcement learning to dynamically allocate more traffic to better-performing variants in real-time. For example, if early data shows "Express Checkout" outperforming "Quick Pay," the AI automatically routes more users to the winning variation while the experiment is still running, maximizing business value (and minimizing loss) while the test is in progress. This adaptive optimization ensures users experience the best version sooner without waiting for manual analysis and decisions.

Building Well-Structured Experiments

Effective experimentation begins with a well-defined hypothesis that aligns with your business objectives and outlines specific, measurable goals. For instance, you might hypothesize that the "Express Checkout" workflow will increase conversion rates by streamlining the payment process. It is important to remember that the purpose of an experiment isn't just to confirm your hypothesis—it's to learn. Early results that contradict your hypothesis aren't failures; these experiments provide valuable insights that may save months of investment in a project unlikely to achieve its goals.

A good experiment ensures that results are meaningful and actionable. It separates feature performance from external factors so that observed outcomes can be attributed solely to the changes being tested. As experimentation scales across teams and products, it's important that experiments are guided by the following criteria.

Strong, clear metrics

Every experiment should begin with a well-defined hypothesis and a key metric that captures what success looks like. For example, if you're testing an "Express Checkout" workflow, your primary metric might be the conversion rate from checkout initiation to completion. Clear metrics focus the experiment, enable measurable progress, and prevent post hoc rationalization. It's equally important to identify guardrail metrics—secondary indicators like error rates or customer churn—that flag unintended side effects and keep you from blindly optimizing a single number at the expense of overall health.

Targeted and randomized audience

Next, focus on targeting your experiment effectively. The ability to tailor experiments for specific user segments—such as by device type, location, or customer tier—is essential. But even within these tailored audiences, randomization must be maintained to avoid biases in results. For example, don't test the same feature on one region versus another without random sampling. This ensures that any observed differences are due to the feature itself, not external factors. And remember, when managing multiple experiments, audience overlap becomes a concern: ensure that users aren't exposed to conflicting experiments that could distort the findings.

A statistically significant sample size and experiment duration

Before running your experiment, calculate the minimum sample size using a power analysis. This helps define how long the experiment needs to run before reliable conclusions can be drawn. An "underpowered" experiment can waste valuable time, as insufficient sample sizes can lead to inconclusive or misleading results. Consider experiment duration carefully: if your results seem inconclusive, having predefined stopping criteria helps you decide when to end an experiment, due to either achieving statistical significance or meeting performance thresholds. This approach prevents wasted effort and ensures the team isn't stuck in endless experiments with ambiguous outcomes.

Experiment separation

In practice, most organizations don't run one experiment at a time. Instead, there may be dozens of live experiments across different parts of the product, which introduces new complexity. Teams must consider test interactions—especially when experiments overlap or target the same users. Well-governed experimentation platforms help by automatically tracking exposure, enforcing mutual exclusivity where needed, and surfacing possible conflicts.

AI-powered interpretation

Modern AI assistants that are integrated into feature management platforms simplify how teams interpret experiment results. Rather than requiring statistical expertise to analyze complex data, AI can interpret results in plain language, explaining the implications of experimental outcomes. For example, when an experiment shows a 5% increase in conversion rates but a slight decrease in average order value, you can ask the AI to explain these trade-offs and their business implications. The AI can analyze multiple metrics simultaneously, identify correlations, and suggest potential relationships that might not be immediately obvious.

To make confident product decisions, we need to trust the insights our experiments provide. By designing experiments with these key elements, we can ensure their reliability and accuracy.

Integrating Experimentation with Progressive Delivery

Just as we progressively roll out new features like "Subscription Payments" to reduce risk, we can use feature flags to implement experiments in a controlled and safe manner. For example, imagine we develop a revised "Subscription Payments" workflow. This iteration aims to simplify the user experience. Our hypothesis is that this version will lead to an increase in subscription sign-ups.

To test this hypothesis, we use feature flags to divide users into two groups: one experiences the original workflow, while the other interacts with the updated version. By randomly assigning users, we ensure a fair comparison and collect reliable data on key metrics, such as sign-up rates and completion times. That approach allows us to evaluate the performance of the new workflow in real-world conditions without exposing the entire user base to potential issues.

If the metrics show that the updated version outperforms the original in driving sign-ups, we can begin gradually rolling it out to a larger percentage of users. The iterative process not only minimizes risk but also ensures that we base our decisions on real data that either confirms or refutes our hypotheses.

Establishing Guardrails

We talked about the importance of identifying a key metric when defining your experiment's hypothesis. It's equally important to identify one or more guardrail metrics.

For example, we worked with a company that matches loan seekers with loan providers. Loan seekers use a sign-up flow to provide information about the type of loan they are interested in along with a number of other details. The service is able to match the user to the loan provider best able to meet their needs.

The product team was confident that a redesigned sign-up flow would improve the quality of the loan matches. They started by carefully rolling this experiment out to a small cohort of users. In rolling out, the team found that the new flow was causing a substantially higher rate of drop-offs, users who navigated away before completing the experiment. A guardrail metric, in this case drop-off rates, helped the team detect in near real time and take action.

By analyzing the data, the product team could then decide what action to take. They could shrink the cohort size or pause wider rollout, which would let them use the experiment to continue to learn about the impact on the goal metric while constraining side effects. Or, the product team could cancel the experiment altogether if they concluded that the side effects were too detrimental to the overall business value.

Guardrail metrics, like drop-off rates in the previous example, serve a different purpose from goal metrics but are equally important in ensuring the success of an experiment. While goal metrics measure the primary objective of the experiment—such as improving conversion rates, increasing revenue, or enhancing user engagement—guardrail metrics act as safety checks to monitor for unintended negative consequences. Example metrics used for guardrails include bounce rate, page load time, customer churn rate, error rate, and conversion rate on secondary product lines.

Guardrail metrics help you maintain a holistic view of the experiment's impact, enabling you to balance progress on the primary goal with the overall health and reliability of the product. By tracking both, you can make informed decisions about when to continue, pause, or pivot their experiments.

The most effective guardrails are automated and seamlessly integrated into the experimentation process. Modern feature management systems can monitor guardrails in real time and enforce thresholds automatically. AI-powered anomaly detection significantly strengthens guardrail monitoring by using ML to identify subtle patterns that might escape human attention. These systems establish baseline metrics behavior and automatically alert when experiment variations cause unexpected deviations, even before they reach predefined thresholds. Additionally, AI can correlate multiple metrics simultaneously to detect complex interactions that simple threshold monitoring would miss.

Automation safeguards your systems by lessening the chance of inadvertently missing performance degradation through human error. Making guardrails a core part of the experimentation process helps payment platforms stay agile while maintaining reliability. This approach ensures that new features can deliver value without risking user trust.

Life Without Mature Feature Management Tools

While feature management systems offer immense value, how effective and cost-efficient they are hangs on their implementation and governance. Relying on fragile, homegrown solutions or multiple decentralized implementations can work against you, particularly as these basic solutions lack the sophisticated AI capabilities that define modern feature management platforms. It's natural for many teams to start by building their own feature management systems when their needs are basic. However, as their needs become more complex, the effort to add more and more capabilities becomes increasingly difficult to justify. The cost of this effort, and the technical debt accrued, eventually outweigh any initial savings. In this section, we'll explore the drawbacks of DIY systems in greater detail.

Low-Quality Tools Impede Effective Feature Flag Management

Feature flags can become liabilities without proper tooling and governance. The challenge lies in the gap between basic feature flag implementation and truly effective feature flag management at scale. As feature flag adoption spreads across teams and projects, first-generation solutions that focus only on simple toggling without measurement, and in-house solutions initially built to solve simple use cases, quickly reveal their limitations. Without sophisticated management capabilities, teams struggle to maintain visibility and control over their growing feature flag ecosystem.

Consider a typical scenario: a development team implements dozens of feature flags across their application using a basic toggle system. While this works initially, they soon discover they can't easily track flag ownership, monitor flag status, or manage flag lifecycles. The system lacks crucial capabilities like AI-powered automated cleanup notifications, usage tracking, or dependency mapping. As a result, developers lose sight of which flags are still needed and which should be retired. The codebase becomes littered with "zombie flags"—permanent toggles that no one dares to remove because they can't determine if the flag is truly obsolete. Additionally, leaving zombie feature flags in place can gate abandoned or obsolete code, which may not be tested or maintained, creating vulnerabilities and increasing technical debt.

Professional-grade feature management tools should provide comprehensive governance features, including clear ownership tracking, automated cleanup processes, dependency visualization, and robust access controls. These capabilities ensure feature flags remain an asset rather than a liability as your system grows in complexity.

Minimal Support for Experimentation Limits Your Learning

Homegrown systems often lack the advanced capabilities required to support high-quality experimentation. For example, while a basic feature flag system might allow you to turn a feature on or off globally, it typically won't support fine-grained targeting by attributes like geography, device type, or customer tier. Similarly, these systems rarely offer true randomized percentage rollouts, where user populations are divided randomly and consistently to ensure fairness and reliability in experiments. Advanced functionality, like using ML to optimize traffic routing, is well beyond the grasp of even the most sophisticated homegrown tools. Without these capabilities, experiments can produce skewed or untrustworthy results.

Additionally, modern experimentation systems include built-in tools for automated statistical analysis and metric tracking, enabling teams to evaluate key performance indicators (KPIs) and guardrail metrics directly within the platform. For instance, if you are testing an updated checkout process on a payment platform, a modern system can automatically calculate conversion rates, identify statistical significance, and flag anomalies like increased error rates—all without manual intervention. Basic systems, by contrast, rely heavily on external tools and manual data aggregation, which increases operational complexity and the risk of errors. This lack of integration and sophistication makes it much harder for teams to experiment effectively, ultimately limiting the potential for data-driven decision making.

Lack of Integrations Slows You Down

Another significant limitation of basic feature management systems is their lack of integration with the broader software development ecosystem, which often results in more hand-offs, manual steps, and complex, hard-to-maintain scripting. Modern feature management systems address these challenges by tightly integrating with critical tools and platforms, embedding feature management seamlessly into your workflows.

Fragile Implementations Distract Your Team

Most notably, DIY systems typically don't scale well. They can be frail and prone to performance bottlenecks. Homegrown solutions often lack formal service-level agreements (SLAs) or dedicated support structures, leading to reduced uptime and reliability. When these systems encounter failures, your teams must devote valuable resources to troubleshooting and resolving disruptions.

Conversely, a robust feature management system helps you deliver business value efficiently and reliably. While building an in-house solution might be an easy way to get started with feature management, these homegrown systems often struggle to meet the evolving needs of high-performing development teams.

The challenges multiply when different teams across an organization develop their own independent feature management implementations. This fragmentation creates unnecessary complexity in several critical areas: managing feature deployments, maintaining security standards, and establishing consistent governance practices across the organization. In the following sections, we'll examine how centralizing feature management through modern, purpose-built tools can streamline operations, enhance security, and improve collaboration across teams.

Scaling Feature Management and Experimentation

Scaling feature management and experimentation requires AI-driven patterns that streamline processes and ensure consistency. In this section we'll look at the advantages of unifying feature management with a single implementation, leveraging smart integrations to reduce manual work and improve collaboration. We'll explore how modern platforms help automate governance, while leveraging your existing identity management infrastructure. We'll understand how modern systems ensure scalability. Finally, we'll see how AI-driven capabilities transform experimentation.

Unify with a Single Feature Management Implementation

We have worked with many large companies that seek to modernize their software delivery processes. In this journey, they are often surprised to discover they're juggling a dozen or more independently built DIY feature management systems, sometimes mixed with partially implemented commercial or open source solutions. As these organizations have grown, their software and delivery processes have become more complex, and the need for a centralized feature management system becomes clear. Fragmented implementations amplify the risk of misconfigurations, security vulnerabilities, and noncompliance. In industries where auditability is critical, these gaps make compliance an uphill battle.

Additionally, maintaining multiple bespoke systems across teams introduces more and more technical debt. The effort and resources required to update, patch, and synchronize these systems detract from delivering business value. Learning how to work with multiple systems is also a tax on developers and product managers when moving between teams.

A centralized feature management implementation gives companies a single, consistent view of feature flags across all environments and allows for safe, consistent feature rollout capabilities across teams. With a unified platform, companies are able to easily track the state of active flags, monitor their usage, and understand dependencies between features. Lack of a unified view can lead to errors during deployment. Dependencies can become tangled, and the very real risk of activating or deactivating flags incorrectly increases, especially as the complexity of systems grows.

AI significantly enhances these integrations by automating contextual decision making. When integrated with CI/CD pipelines, AI can automatically detect which feature flags are impacted by specific code changes, helping ensure that proper testing occurs before deployment.

Reduce Manual Steps with Smart Integrations

Modern systems streamline workflows by embedding feature management directly into the broader software ecosystem. Integrations with integrated development environments (IDEs) allow developers to create and manage feature flags directly within their coding environment, reducing context switching and streamlining the development process. CI/CD pipeline integrations enable teams to incorporate feature flags into automated build and deployment processes, allowing feature flags to become a natural part of them.

Similarly, connections to task management, notification, and approval platforms like Jira, Slack, Microsoft Teams, and ServiceNow ensure that feature flag changes can be tracked, approved, and communicated in real time, keeping stakeholders informed and reducing miscommunication.

With basic feature management systems, the configuration of the feature flags themselves is a key cause of developer toil. Implementing feature flags and experiments traditionally requires developers to carefully configure SDKs, write targeting rules, and ensure proper tracking of metrics. Modern AI systems address this issue since they can generate this implementation code automatically based on your experiment configuration. Here's what makes it particularly powerful: with coding assistants integrated into your IDE, the AI understands the context of your experiment and can generate code that's tailored to your use case.

For instance, if you've configured an experiment to test a new checkout flow for premium users in certain geographic regions, the AI can generate all the necessary code for your chosen programming language. This includes:

- Injecting the feature flag into your code with the proper syntax and API key
- Implementing any needed experiment tracking telemetry
- Handling edge cases and error conditions

The AI adapts its code generation to match your specific needs and can explain its implementation choices. If you need to modify the generated code or implement it in a different programming language, you can simply ask the AI to regenerate it with your new requirements. This dramatically reduces the time from experiment design to implementation while ensuring consistent, high-quality code.

By eliminating manual scripting and enabling automation across these tools, built-in integrations create workflows that not only reduce toil but also improve collaboration, efficiency, and agility.

Simplify Governance with Automated Audit Trails and Enforcement

Modern feature management systems simplify governance by automating crucial processes such as approvals and policy enforcement, which helps your teams maintain control while reducing operational overhead. For example, you can set up automated workflows to require mandatory approvals for any feature flag changes in production, and require that those flags have been activated in test environments first. Doing so ensures that sensitive environments are protected from unintended or risky modifications, while allowing more flexibility in development or staging, where experimentation and iteration are more common. This differentiation in enforcement balances working efficiency with production stability.

Policies within these systems can also help standardize practices across teams. For instance, consistent flag naming conventions can be enforced automatically, making it easier for teams to understand the purpose of a flag at a glance, even as the number of flags grows. Additionally, modern systems can guide flags through a defined promotion lifecycle, ensuring that temporary flags used for testing or experiments are properly retired once they're no longer needed. For high-stakes changes, such as deployments in production, these systems can mandate the use of golden pipelines—predefined, validated processes that ensure rigorous testing and reliable rollouts. By automating these governance tasks, modern systems eliminate ambiguity, align teams with organizational standards, and significantly reduce the likelihood of misconfigurations that could jeopardize reliability or security.

Leverage Your Existing Identity Management Infrastructure

Modern feature systems support single sign-on (SSO), allowing your team to use existing credentials from in-house identity providers, and a system for cross-domain identity management (SCIM) simplifies user provisioning and role assignments, ensuring that the right accounts and permissions exist across systems. Along with RBAC, you can enforce consistent governance, ensuring that only authorized users can adjust feature flags or modify settings. This ensures every user has the privileges needed for their role when they need it, no more and no less, reducing the likelihood of security breaches and compliance violations. Together, SSO and SCIM enhance governance, streamline onboarding and offboarding, and ensure secure, consistent access control across teams.

Choose a Platform Built to Scale

Modern systems are built with scalability and reliability at their core. They leverage content delivery networks and other features of low-latency, high-availability architectures to maintain performance under peak loads, which can grow significantly over time as user bases and system complexity increase. These systems also employ push architectures to propagate configuration updates instantly across environments, enabling features like near-instant rollbacks or real-time targeting changes. By incorporating other best practices for mission-critical applications, such as redundancy and fault tolerance, modern systems ensure that feature management remains robust and responsive, even during periods of heavy traffic or unexpected demand spikes.

Summary

This chapter explored how feature management and experimentation serve as foundational elements of modern software delivery, enabling teams to deploy code more frequently while maintaining stability through progressive rollouts and robust rollback capabilities. We learned that feature flags not only help manage deployment risk but also drive business value through experimentation, allowing teams to make data-driven decisions based on real user behavior rather than speculation. Additionally, we saw how modern feature management platforms overcome the limitations of homegrown solutions by providing comprehensive governance, scalability, and AI-powered capabilities that make experimentation more accessible and insightful.

As we turn to cloud cost management in Chapter 9, we'll explore another critical aspect of operating at scale: understanding and optimizing the financial implications of our architectural and operational decisions in cloud environments, where the flexibility that enables rapid feature delivery and experimentation must be balanced against resource efficiency and cost-effectiveness.

CHAPTER 9

AI and Automation
for Cloud Cost Management

It's hard to overstate how important cloud environments and effective cloud cost management strategies are to modern organizations. In 2025, companies worldwide will spend an astonishing $723.4 billion on public cloud services, according to Gartner projections. This represents a significant jump from $595.7 billion in 2024. Cloud environments and services have become central to modern software delivery, and cloud spending has become a substantial line item in IT budgets.

Managing these growing costs has become a complex problem. Recent industry estimates suggest that 30% of cloud spending is wasted. The reasons are numerous: organizations often provision more cloud resources than they actually need, leading to unused or underutilized instances and forgotten services, which still incur costs.

In this chapter, we'll jump into the thorny problem of cloud cost management. We'll look at how practices have evolved from the early days of cloud computing, giving rise to the discipline of FinOps (financial operations). Since carbon footprint and cloud cost management are interconnected, we'll look into how cloud cost management leads to environmental sustainability initiatives.

We'll also explore how AI-powered solutions are addressing the challenges of unpredictable spending, time-consuming optimization tasks, and the complexities of multicloud governance. We will look at specific AI-driven strategies for optimizing cloud resources, such as leveraging cost-effective pricing models and managing containerized environments. Furthermore, we'll explore how AI can power cloud governance and compliance to ensure that your organization's cloud investments are both efficient and secure.

The Evolution of Cloud Cost Management

We'll start by exploring how cloud cost management has changed over time and we'll look at how FinOps provides a framework to address the challenges of cloud cost management. Finally, we'll look at the importance of automation in FinOps.

Early Cloud Adoption and Initial Challenges

In the precloud era, organizations typically owned and maintained their own on-premises infrastructure requiring significant up-front investments (capital expenditures) in hardware and software. IT budgets were typically fixed and tied to the depreciation cycles of these assets, which created a rigid framework. While costs were predictable, this model was difficult to adapt to changing business demands.

Cloud computing, with on-demand, pay-as-you-go IT resources, flipped this model. Spending went from capital expenditures to operational expenses, with costs spread out over time based on actual usage. This provided a greater ability to respond to market changes, scale operations, and avoid overprovisioning, but pay-as-you-use brought new challenges. Early adopters of cloud services often faced unexpected costs due to this model. Limited visibility into how cloud resources were being used created new challenges, and keeping costs in check was a struggle.

The Rise of FinOps

Early cloud pioneers developed their own cost optimization practices to address the challenges of managing cloud spending. Cloudability, an early cloud cost management platform, fostered a community around these challenges, leading to the formalization of the term "FinOps" with the creation of the FinOps Foundation in 2019.

FinOps practices emphasize collaboration and shared ownership of cloud costs, as well as individual and team accountability for cloud usage and its associated costs. The key to FinOps is reliance on data and reporting to understand cloud spending patterns and identify optimization opportunities. As with DevOps, an ethos of continuous improvement is important to FinOps. FinOps practices are meant to be ongoing with iterative optimization of cloud usage and costs over time.

Core principles of FinOps

The FinOps Foundation defines six core principles (*https://oreil.ly/zxPsZ*) to help an organization manage cloud costs. Here's a breakdown:

Teams need to collaborate
> FinOps encourages close collaboration between technology, finance, and business teams to foster a shared understanding of cloud costs and how they relate to

business goals. Developers, engineers, and product managers are empowered to make informed decisions about their cloud usage and contribute to optimization efforts.

Decisions are driven by the business value of the cloud
Cloud spending decisions should be driven by the value they bring to the business, not solely by cost considerations. FinOps encourages understanding the cost of delivering a product or service in the cloud, enabling better pricing strategies and investment decisions.

Everyone takes ownership of their cloud usage
Individuals and teams are accountable for the cloud resources they consume and the associated costs. This empowers teams to make responsible choices about their cloud usage and contribute to cost optimization efforts.

FinOps data should be accessible and timely
Cloud spending data should be readily accessible and up-to-date, enabling timely analysis and decision making. Organizations should leverage data analysis and reporting to understand cloud spending patterns and identify optimization opportunities.

A centralized team drives FinOps
A dedicated FinOps team, often led by a FinOps practitioner, drives the implementation and ongoing refinement of FinOps practices. This team handles rate optimizations while maintaining a shared accountability model that allows engineering teams to focus solely on optimizing their environment usage.

Teams take advantage of the variable cost model of the cloud
FinOps encourages leveraging the variable cost model of the cloud to scale resources up or down as needed, aligning spending with business demands. This principle emphasizes using cloud-native tools and strategies to optimize costs, such as right-sizing resources, leveraging discounts, and automating cost-saving measures.

Phases of FinOps

The three phases of FinOps—Inform, Optimize, and Operate—provide a framework for organizations to progressively improve their cloud financial management. Here's a closer look at each phase.

Inform.   This phase focuses on gaining visibility into your cloud spending and usage patterns. In this phase, we ask questions like:

What are we spending on the cloud?
This involves gathering data from various sources, including cloud provider billing systems, to create a centralized view of your cloud costs.

Where is the money going?
> This requires allocating costs to specific departments, projects, or business units. Tagging resources and using cost allocation tools are crucial for this step.

How are we using cloud resources?
> This involves analyzing usage patterns to understand how different teams and services contribute to overall cloud expenses.

As part of this investigation, we may create reports and dashboards to visualize spending patterns and identify trends. We are also interested in anomaly detection, using tools to identify unusual spending spikes or anomalies that require further investigation.

Optimize.   Once we have an understanding of our cloud spending, it's time to optimize. This phase focuses on identifying and implementing cost-saving measures:

Right-sizing resources
> Analyze resource utilization and adjust instance sizes, storage tiers, and other configurations to match actual needs.

Leveraging discounts
> Take advantage of discounts offered by cloud providers. We'll look more at this in the next section.

Automating cost optimization
> Use automation tools to schedule instance shutdowns, optimize resource allocation, and enforce cost policies.

Eliminating waste
> Identify and eliminate unused or underutilized resources, such as idle instances, orphaned volumes, and unattached storage.

Operate.   The Operate phase is about establishing ongoing processes for managing and monitoring cloud costs. We embed FinOps practices into our culture and workflows:

Budgeting and forecasting
> Set clear budgets for cloud spending and use forecasting tools to predict future costs.

Continuous monitoring
> Track cloud spending and usage patterns on an ongoing basis to identify any deviations from budget or unexpected spikes.

Automate cost optimization

Automate common tasks by implementing scripts or using cloud provider tools to handle routine activities like resource cleanup, right-sizing, and reservation management.

By iterating through these three phases repeatedly, optimization is an ongoing project.

Modern Cloud Cost Management Challenges

As cloud environments grow more complex with multicloud and hybrid infrastructures, traditional cost management approaches become inadequate. Modern strategies are required to effectively navigate and control the increasing cloud spending in these environments.

A 2023 study by 451 Research (*https://oreil.ly/8oLC3*), commissioned by Oracle Cloud Infrastructure, found that 98% of enterprises use or plan to use at least two cloud infrastructure providers. In addition, 31% of enterprises are using four or more cloud infrastructure providers. A multicloud or hybrid approach helps prevent single-vendor reliance and gives companies the freedom to select best-in-breed services from various providers based on their specific strengths.

A multicloud or hybrid approach also minimizes the impact of outages by distributing workloads across multiple clouds. This approach can also help companies comply with data sovereignty laws that dictate data storage locations. In addition, the ability to cherry-pick the most cost-effective services and pricing models from different providers unlocks significant opportunities for optimizing cloud spending.

In addition to increasing operational complexity, managing cloud costs across multicloud or hybrid environments brings distinct challenges. Each cloud provider has its own billing system with different formats, metrics, and reporting tools. This makes it difficult to get a consolidated view of spending across all platforms, particularly when cost data is siloed within different departments or teams. In addition, cloud providers have complex pricing models that can be difficult to compare across platforms. This makes it challenging to allocate costs accurately to specific projects, departments, or business units.

AI-Driven Cloud Cost Optimization Strategies

AI can help you take control of your cloud spending. The technology's strength lies in its ability to process the vast amounts of data generated, identifying patterns and anomalies that would be nearly impossible for humans to detect. Applied to cloud computing cost management, AI can not only give us insights into current spending, but also predict future cloud usage with remarkable accuracy. AI algorithms, such as long short-term memory (LSTM) and bidirectional LSTM networks and decision tree regression (*https://oreil.ly/ZUDAh*), can forecast compute needs weeks or even months in advance. In this section, we'll look at practical strategies to reduce your cloud bill without impacting performance, and we'll explore how AI can help you right-size resources, leverage discounts, and automate cost controls, all while supporting your business goals.

Right-Sizing Cloud Resources

Right-sizing is at the dead center of responsible cloud cost management. This is the practice of optimizing cloud resource allocation to match the actual needs of your applications and workloads. Right-sizing is a critical strategy that involves ensuring that you're neither underprovisioning (which can lead to performance issues) nor overprovisioning (which can lead to unnecessary costs). Teams often start by deploying a service or application and allocating more resources than needed out of concern for poor performance. Without accurate usage data, it can be difficult to estimate precise requirements. Misconfigured automated scaling can also contribute to excessive resource allocation.

While compute resources (VMs and containers) are often the initial focus of right-sizing efforts, they also apply to other cloud resources, including:

Storage
> Right-sizing involves selecting the appropriate storage tiers and volumes based on usage patterns. This covers block storage (like Amazon EBS or Google Persistent Disk), file storage, and object storage (such as Amazon S3 or Google Cloud Storage).

Databases
> Right-sizing involves selecting the right database instance types, storage configurations, and database performance and capacity to reduce costs.

Network
> Right-sizing includes optimizing the use of network resources like load balancers, VPN gateways, and bandwidth. Right-sizing can help minimize unnecessary costs associated with overprovisioned network resources.

Cloud cost visibility required for the FinOps Inform phase

Effective optimization requires understanding both your resource utilization patterns and the associated costs. This is where the FinOps Inform phase comes in. To gain a precise understanding of cloud costs, engineers must have access to detailed cloud analytics that highlight how resources—compute, storage, memory, and others—are being used and how they map to actual spending.

This can be complex. Often costs are managed by finance teams, and engineers may not even have access to financial data. If they do, they may have limited insight into how their cloud resources actually translate into dollars and cents. The challenge lies in providing engineers with clear, concise, and actionable visibility into the costs associated with the specific resources their applications are consuming. This can be particularly difficult with complex, multiapplication, or multitenant cloud environments, where costs can be distributed across many resources.

Modern cloud cost management tools, such as Harness CCM and various cloud provider tools, help bridge this divide by offering self-service visibility to engineers, enabling them to see the real costs of their applications, microservices, clusters, and environments. These tools empower engineers by giving them the context they need to manage cloud costs directly, without relying on finance or operations teams to provide that information. Unlike traditional systems, which are limited to basic infrastructure views, modern tools integrate with cloud services and provide detailed, application-level cost data.

Moving from Inform to Optimize

Once you have a clear understanding of your cloud usage and costs, you are ready to move on to the Optimize phase of FinOps. You can make data-driven decisions about how to adjust your cloud resources to be more efficient and cost-effective. With the visibility into costs and usage patterns, you can confidently make changes that align with both performance and budgetary constraints.

AI-powered tools are becoming indispensable here, eliminating the need to manually monitor and adjust resources to meet demand. With continuous monitoring and features like idle resource detection and resource usage analysis, tools can help identify inefficiencies and recommend adjustments or automatically make adjustments to CPU, memory, and storage configurations.

Optimization, however, should be approached gradually. Start with small, incremental changes, and continuously refine your strategy based on observed impacts. AI-powered tools can help by predicting how to adjust resources by forecasting usage into the future and using past small changes as feedback to make subsequent fine-tuning actions. This iterative process is a key aspect of the Operate phase of FinOps. By fine-tuning your cloud environment in this way, you can validate performance requirements, ensuring that your application runs efficiently without sacrificing user experience or application performance.

Leveraging Commitment-Based Pricing and Spot Instances

Leveraging commitment-based pricing models and spot instances are additional strategies to reduce cloud costs.

Commitment-based pricing involves pledging a specific level of cloud resource usage over a defined period in exchange for significant discounts. Offered by major cloud providers like AWS, Microsoft Azure, and Google Cloud, these models—commonly referred to as Reserved Instances or Committed Use Contracts—can deliver savings of up to 80%, compared with on-demand pricing. Longer commitments (typically one to three years) and higher up-front payments yield the largest discounts. AWS's Reserved Instances, for example, offer discounts of 30% to 72% on compute resources, while Google Cloud's Committed Use Contracts provide similar savings on compute, storage, and other services. These offerings are ideal for predictable workloads, such as steady-state applications, but require accurate usage forecasting to avoid over- or underprovisioning.

Spot instances, on the other hand, provide a dynamic way to cut costs by utilizing unused cloud capacity at steep discounts—up to 90% less than on-demand prices. These instances are ideal for noncritical, flexible workloads, such as batch processing, data analysis, or development environments, as they can be interrupted with minimal notice. By combining commitment-based pricing for stable workloads and spot instances for flexible or transient tasks, businesses can achieve a powerful balance of cost efficiency and operational flexibility. Advanced tools and AI-driven forecasting can help organizations navigate these models effectively, ensuring optimal resource allocation and maximum cost savings.

Key considerations

When leveraging commitment-based pricing models and spot instances to optimize cloud costs, you need to consider their unique advantages and challenges to maximize their value while mitigating potential risks.

Commitment-based pricing models are ideal for predictable, steady workloads. However, they require accurate forecasting of resource usage over extended periods, typically one to three years. Misjudging usage can lead to overcommitting, resulting in underutilized resources and wasted costs, or undercommitting, which may lead to higher on-demand charges. Flexibility is also limited, as these commitments lock businesses into specific instance types, regions, or service tiers, depending on the provider. To address these challenges, you must establish practices to:

- Analyze historical usage data to improve forecasting accuracy.
- Use convertible or flexible options, when available, to adjust commitments as needs change.
- Regularly monitor and optimize resource usage to align with commitments.

The transient nature of spot instances, which can be terminated with little notice, requires careful planning and workload adaptation. You must:

- Ensure that workloads can tolerate interruptions without significant impact.

- Implement checkpointing or automated job recovery mechanisms to minimize disruptions.

- Monitor market trends to predict spot instance availability and pricing fluctuations.

A hybrid strategy combining commitment-based pricing for steady workloads and spot instances for flexible tasks can offer the best of both worlds: predictable cost savings and dynamic scaling at low prices. To implement a hybrid strategy effectively, your practices must:

- Evaluate workload characteristics to determine the appropriate mix of commitment-based resources and spot capacity.

- Leverage automation tools, such as cloud-native autoscaling and workload orchestration systems, to optimize usage.

- Continuously assess and refine the strategy to adapt to changing business needs and workload patterns.

How AI can help

Clearly, optimizing between commitment-based pricing models and spot instances quickly gets complex. Modern AI tools, including GenAI, can help overcome these challenges with accurate forecasting, dynamic optimization, and seamless automation.

For commitment-based pricing, AI agents, such as the Harness FinOps Agent, can analyze historical usage patterns and predict future resource needs with precision, reducing the risks of over- or undercommitting. AI tools can also identify the ideal mix of reserved and on-demand resources while continuously monitoring and adjusting commitments to align with changing workloads. Additionally, AI systems can detect anomalies in resource consumption, ensuring businesses avoid inefficiencies or penalties.

For spot instance optimization, AI can address their unpredictability by forecasting availability and pricing trends, enabling smarter scheduling for interruption-tolerant workloads. AI-powered workload orchestration tools automate the deployment and scaling of tasks, dynamically shifting them to alternative resources when spot instances are interrupted. Moreover, AI optimizes checkpointing and recovery processes, ensuring workloads can resume efficiently while minimizing downtime. This is particularly valuable for tasks like batch processing or data analytics.

By integrating both models, AI can create an intelligent hybrid strategy that balances the cost efficiency of reserved resources with the flexibility and low pricing of spot instances. It ensures optimal resource allocation based on workload requirements, predicts demand surges to adjust resources proactively, and provides actionable insights for continuous cost optimization.

Using AI to Manage Container Costs

Containerized architectures play an important role in modern application development. *Containers* package applications and their dependencies into lightweight, portable units, enabling them to run consistently across different environments. These containers operate on *nodes*, which are physical or virtual machines (often referred to as instances) that provide the underlying resources. Multiple nodes combine to form a *cluster*, a coordinated group of machines that work together to run and manage containers. Within a node, containers are typically grouped into *pods*, which share resources and are deployed together as a single operational unit. The management of these clusters is handled through *orchestration*, where tools like Kubernetes automate the deployment, scaling, and lifecycle management of containers.

While containerized architectures offer unmatched portability, resource efficiency, and adaptability across diverse environments, managing cloud costs for containerized environments is different from managing costs in VM environments. The shared underlying infrastructure complicates cost tracking. In VM environments, each virtual machine is a stand-alone unit with fixed resources, so costs are easier to allocate. However, when multiple containers run on a single server instance, your cloud bill will provide only the usage of the underlying server, not individual containers. This makes it difficult to accurately understand the usage costs between the containers, as you need more detailed information about how resources like CPU and memory are being shared. The lack of visibility presents challenges in cost attribution, making it harder to track and manage expenses at the container level.

Containerization does not eliminate the need for FinOps; the same principles of financial accountability and cost optimization remain crucial for containerized applications. Unless you rely on cloud-managed container platforms, you must gather supplemental data about how server resources are utilized by running containers. This includes tracking the proportions of CPU, memory, and storage that each container consumes on shared server instances. Pairing this granular resource usage data with your cloud billing information enables accurate cost allocation, ensuring teams and applications are held accountable for their resource consumption. Without this level of insight, it becomes challenging to manage and optimize costs effectively in a containerized environment.

AI again can play an important role. One of the key ways AI helps is through intelligent resource allocation: it analyzes historical usage patterns and workloads to predict resource requirements for containers, suggesting optimal configurations for pods, scaling policies, and node sizes. This reduces overprovisioning, so containers have just the resources they need without wasting capacity. Additionally, AI enables dynamic workload scaling, automatically scaling down workloads during periods of low usage, which complements the Kubernetes autoscaling functionality to maximize cost savings.

AI also improves cost control through forecasting and alerts. By analyzing historical usage and identifying trends, AI models can predict future Kubernetes-related costs, providing accurate projections that help teams plan budgets effectively. Alerts can notify stakeholders of potential budget overruns, enabling corrective action before costs spiral out of control. Moreover, AI can intelligently schedule workloads across clusters, nodes, or even regions to minimize cloud spend while maintaining performance, compliance, and reliability.

Aligning Cost Savings Goals with Business Objectives

While AI can make it easier to find cost savings, keep in mind the FinOps principle that decisions are driven by the business value of the cloud. It's critical that we weigh cloud cost savings against our business requirements for quality, speed, and innovation.

Consider a large retail company preparing to launch a new platform before a peak sales season. Its primary goal is to ensure a smooth and successful launch, even if it means higher initial cloud costs. The increased revenue of an on-time and flawless launch, providing an excellent customer experience, may outweigh the immediate need to minimize cloud costs. The retailer might accept higher initial expenses to ensure a successful launch, knowing that it can optimize cloud usage and reduce costs in the long run.

While cost savings are a crucial consideration, remember, it's equally important to invest strategically to maximize business benefits. Factors such as enabling rapid scaling to accelerate growth, increase revenue, speed up delivery times, improve customer satisfaction, and reduce labor costs should all be considered along with the expenditure.

Automating Cloud Governance and Compliance

So far, we've explored the core principles of FinOps and looked at tactical approaches for optimizing your cloud resources, from right-sizing and leveraging discounts to managing containerized environments. But how do you ensure these practices are consistently applied and aligned with your organization's broader goals? That's where cloud cost governance comes in. Cloud governance frameworks are sets of policies, procedures, and best practices that define how an organization uses and manages its cloud resources. Think of these as a blueprint for secure and efficient cloud adoption and cost management. In this section, we will examine how a robust governance framework ties together the various aspects of cloud financial management. Lastly, we'll look at the role automation and AI can play in enforcing governance policies.

Implementing Cloud Governance Policies

Setting clear goals for your cloud strategy is the first step to creating a solid cloud cost governance framework. This helps ensure your cloud operations align with business priorities like managing costs, driving innovation, and supporting growth. Specific success metrics tied to your strategy could include reducing cloud waste by 20%, achieving 95% tagging compliance, or limiting monthly cost variances to 5%.

An effective governance policy should cover areas including:

Cost visibility
> This encompasses considerations such as your resource tagging policy, which we will look at in detail in the next section. Cost visibility policy can also include configuration of alerts for unexpected cost spikes, using tools such as Google Cloud Billing or custom scripts integrated with Slack or email notifications.

Budgeting and forecasting
> A policy should set team-specific budgets with a buffer for unforeseen growth.

Optimization processes
> A policy should include optimization practices such as regularly analyzing resource usage and adjusting instance sizes to better match workloads, pre-purchase of reserved or savings plans for predictable workloads, and use of spot instances for fault-tolerant workloads to reduce compute expenses.

Security and compliance
> Lastly, a policy should implement RBAC to limit resource access based on user roles. Automate checks to ensure compliance with regulations like GDPR or HIPAA using tools like Prisma Cloud or AWS Security Hub.

AI and automation make it easier to enforce policies automatically, reducing the chance of mistakes or oversights. For example, AI-powered tools can add or check tags on resources and send real-time alerts if policies aren't followed. These tools can also help in analyzing the infrastructure and suggesting policies that can be set up to improve the overall cost, security, and compliance posture. Additionally, they help avoid unexpected cost spikes by flagging unusual activity and ensuring that systems remain compliant without constant manual checks.

Automation also simplifies processes that are prone to human error, like setting up access controls or allocating resources. By automating these tasks, you can reduce the risk of security issues and improve how smoothly your cloud environment runs. Combining automation with clear policies ensures that cloud usage stays cost-efficient, secure, and aligned with the organization's goals.

Enforcing Budget Guardrails with Automation

Automation is essential in enforcing budget guardrails, especially in environments with dynamic resource allocation. Budget overruns are often caused by the uncontrolled proliferation of resources, unexpected usage spikes, or failure to monitor costs in real time. Mechanisms to monitor, alert, and act when spending thresholds are approached can automatically enforce policies such as shutting down underutilized resources, scaling down instances, or restricting new resource provisioning once spending nears predefined limits. This ensures that costs remain within financial goals without relying solely on manual interventions, which are prone to delays and errors.

AI can take this even further by predicting when costs might go over budget before it happens. The technology can forecast when spending will exceed the budget and take automatic steps to prevent it. For example, an AI system might see that a certain project's cloud resource usage is growing quickly and predict that it will go over the budget by the end of the month. The system can then act, perhaps by adjusting resources to cheaper options or notifying the team to make adjustments. For instance, during a big sales event, AI could ensure that the needed resources are in place without letting the costs spiral, automatically balancing cost and performance. AI tools can potentially correlate external business metrics like sales data, headcount, and industry market movements and factor them into the forecasting engine alongside historical usage patterns and correlations to these external factors.

Ensuring Tag Compliance Through Automation

Cost allocation is fundamental to cloud cost management, as it provides transparency into how cloud resources are being consumed and by whom. Accurately attributing costs to specific teams, projects, or applications creates accountability and encourages responsible cloud usage. This transparency ensures that every team is part of cost optimization efforts.

Tagging is key to cost allocation. Tags are metadata labels attached to cloud resources, providing information about their purpose and ownership. You might, for example, use an Environment tag set to Production, Development, or Testing to differentiate resource usage by stage. You might use a Cost Center tag to link resources to business units or budgets. Cloud accounts are another tool for cost allocation. By creating a tiered system of accounts—typically with a root account overseeing child accounts for different environments, teams, or projects—you can centralize billing and governance while maintaining individual account flexibility. Tags combined with cloud account hierarchies enable accurate tracking and allocation of costs. For instance, tagging a VM with relevant details allows for easy filtering and analysis of cloud bills to understand spending patterns by project, department, or application.

An effective tagging strategy should be comprehensive and easily understood across the organization. The strategy should define the key information to track, such as project names, departments, and application names, and use clear, concise, and consistent tag names.

The right tooling is required to ensure the consistent use of the tags you require. Manual tagging can fall short, especially across complex multicloud environments. Human error can lead to inconsistencies, missing tags, or incorrect values, hindering cost allocation and resource tracking. Automation here can enforce tagging policies and validate tag values across all cloud platforms.

Automated tools can also audit tags regularly to identify and fix or report noncompliant resources, ensuring uniformity and accuracy across your entire cloud estate. This not only saves time and reduces errors but also strengthens your cloud governance and cost optimization efforts. AI can also help in normalizing multiple tag variations that are similar into a consolidated tag variation, reducing noise.

Allocating the Costs of Shared Platforms and Services

Another challenge to cost allocation is the use of shared platforms and services, a common feature of modern cloud architectures. When infrastructure or resources are shared across teams and applications, it becomes more complex to divide costs accurately. Modern, AI-powered tools excel at attributing costs based on resource usage patterns and dependencies.

Cloud Cost Management to Meet Environmental Sustainability Goals

As organizations migrate to the cloud, aligning cost management strategies with sustainability goals can help you both reduce operational expenses and decrease your environmental impact. Beyond the typical focus on just saving money, a green approach to cloud cost management also involves actively choosing eco-friendly options and tracking your environmental footprint. The following practices illustrate how to achieve these dual benefits:

Right-sizing and optimizing cloud resources
    Continuously monitor cloud usage to identify and eliminate underutilized or idle resources. Right-sizing ensures that only necessary resources are provisioned, which reduces both costs and energy consumption. Implement autoscaling mechanisms to adjust resource allocation based on real-time demand, preventing overprovisioning and unnecessary energy use. You can also implement auto-stopping to turn off resources that are not being used, thus achieving a zero-carbon footprint for them.

Leverage renewable energy and green cloud providers

Choose cloud service providers that operate data centers powered by renewable energy. For example, Google Cloud Platform has some regions that use 100% renewable energy (*https://oreil.ly/R6bQM*), enabling organizations to reduce their carbon footprint through eco-friendly infrastructure choices. You should also prioritize providers and regions with lower carbon intensity.

Implement cost allocation and accountability

Allocate cloud costs to each department, project, or team to increase visibility and encourage responsible resource usage. This not only optimizes spending but also promotes accountability for sustainability efforts. Use tagging, standardized workflows, and automated governance policies to ensure resources are used efficiently and in compliance with sustainability objectives.

Adopt energy-efficient workload scheduling

Schedule nonurgent or batch workloads to run during off-peak hours or in regions with lower energy costs and carbon intensity, further reducing both spend and emissions. Utilize AI-driven tools to analyze usage patterns and recommend optimal workload placement for both cost and environmental efficiency.

Integrate sustainability metrics into cloud strategy

Build "green teams" responsible for setting and tracking sustainability goals such as greenhouse gas emissions, energy consumption, and water use. You can also incorporate sustainability KPIs into cloud management dashboards (such as the ones provided by AWS) and gamify sustainability efforts to motivate teams to find innovative ways to reduce both costs and environmental impact.

Track carbon footprint

Use cloud management platforms that offer carbon tracking features to measure the environmental impact of cloud usage and generate carbon offsets. Tools like Cloud Carbon Footprint and Harness Cloud Cost Management provide organizations with best-case estimates to measure, monitor, and reduce cloud spending and associated carbon emissions. You can also reinvent savings from cloud cost optimization as investments in carbon credits or other eco-friendly initiatives, turning financial efficiency into measurable climate action.

By combining these strategies, organizations can correlate cost savings directly with sustainability goals. This approach not only enhances operational and financial performance but also demonstrates a clear commitment to environmental stewardship in the digital era.

The Future of AI in Cloud Cost Management

Cloud cost management tools are rapidly evolving to leverage AI insights to simplify the work of optimizing cloud usage. We see a future in which AI powers cloud cost management with innovative new functionality.

As an example, natural language interfaces and conversational AI hold promise for making cloud cost management even more accessible. Emerging interfaces will enable users to interact with complex systems in simple, conversational ways. Instead of navigating dashboards or interpreting detailed reports, users can ask questions like, "What's driving my cloud spend this month?" or "Which services are over budget?" and receive clear, actionable answers. This reduces the technical barrier for nontechnical stakeholders and empowers teams across the organization to engage with cloud cost data. For example, a FinOps practitioner might use a conversational AI tool integrated into Slack or Microsoft Teams to request, "Show me the top five projects exceeding their budgets," and instantly receive a list along with recommendations for optimization.

We also see a growing role for AI in balancing cost savings while minimizing the environmental impact of cloud usage. Optimizing workloads, right-sizing resources, and using energy-efficient cloud regions can often achieve both goals, though sustainability efforts may sometimes require up-front investments. AWS, Google Cloud, and Azure already offer tools such as the Customer Carbon Footprint Tool, Carbon Sense Suite, and Sustainability Calculator to gain insights into the carbon impact of cloud usage.

These are just a few examples of the features AI will bring to helping us manage our cloud usage. Cloud services are both powerful and complex. Using AI and modern tools, now and in the future, will help you optimize resource allocation, leverage cost-effective pricing models, and achieve greater financial control and sustainability in the cloud.

Summary

Managing cloud costs has become an increasingly complex and pressing issue for organizations as cloud expenditures surge across industries. The shift from traditional on-premises infrastructure to cloud-based environments has brought greater agility and scalability, but it has also introduced new layers of cost unpredictability and operational complexity. In response, the FinOps discipline has emerged, emphasizing cross-functional collaboration, shared accountability, and the use of real-time data to optimize cloud spending and maximize business value.

Modern strategies leverage AI and automation to address issues like resource over-provisioning, multicloud complexity, and cost allocation, enabling practices such as right-sizing, leveraging commitment-based pricing and spot instances, and managing containerized environments efficiently. AI-powered tools improve visibility, forecasting, and enforcement of governance policies. They automate tasks such as tagging, anomaly detection, and budget guardrails to ensure cost control, compliance, and alignment with business and sustainability objectives. Integrating AI and automation into cloud cost management ultimately empowers organizations to optimize spending, improve operational efficiency, and support environmental sustainability initiatives.

CHAPTER 10

A Platform Engineering Approach to Modern DevOps

The previous chapters have painted a picture of the many systems and practices that characterize modern software delivery. This long journey has illustrated the daunting complexity that modern software teams must contend with. In addition, modern software development has tended to "shift left" many concerns—security, observability, and infrastructure management work—that were previously handled by operations teams. If even the most experienced and well-resourced development teams are strained by this complexity and added responsibility, how are we to manage?

Platform engineering has emerged to help modern software organizations answer this very question. It is the discipline of designing, building, and maintaining internal developer platforms that provide integrated tooling and infrastructure for software delivery. While previous chapters explored the individual components of modern software delivery, we'll see in this chapter how platform engineering pulls these capabilities together into a cohesive platform that serves development teams.

In this chapter, we'll explore how organizations can build and run effective platform engineering teams. We'll look at how these teams fit into organizations and what role they play in enabling rapid, secure delivery. Then we'll dig into the practical aspects of building and operating high-performing platform teams—everything from team structure to day-to-day operations. We'll explore concrete ways to measure developer platform effectiveness, ensuring our investments deliver real value. We'll discuss the balance between standardization and team autonomy—how to provide guardrails without stifling innovation. Finally, we'll look at strategies for sustainable platform evolution, ensuring our platform grows alongside our organization's needs.

Why Platform Engineering?

We understand that traditional approaches to developer tooling often require development teams to navigate a complex landscape of tools and practices on their own. Platform engineering treats internal developer platforms as a strategic product, with development teams as valued customers. This shift comes at a critical time, as the rapid evolution of software practices has created a cognitive load crisis for developers, who must juggle an expanding set of responsibilities. Platform engineering addresses this crisis, and we'll dig into the business case for it and how it reinforces a collaborative DevOps culture.

The Developer Cognitive Load Crisis

Each new tool that we add to our toolchain and each new practice we add to our delivery process promises to accelerate delivery or to improve software quality. The cumulative effect, however, can create an unsustainable cognitive burden on our development teams. Consider that developers must juggle SCM, CI/CD pipeline configuration, IaC templates, security scanning tools, deployment strategies, monitoring systems, and a host of other specialized tools. Each comes with its own complexities, best practices, and failure modes.

This cognitive burden is particularly acute as teams adopt AI-powered tools across the development lifecycle. While these tools promise to accelerate delivery, they often require significant expertise to implement effectively. Platform engineering can encapsulate this complexity, making AI capabilities accessible through standardized interfaces and templates, without requiring every developer to become an AI expert.

The data tells a concerning story: a recent Harness survey (*https://oreil.ly/TyQ9U*) of engineering leaders found that 78% of developers spend at least 30% of their time on manual, repetitive tasks rather than writing code. Hours get consumed by operational responsibilities and tool management—activities that, while necessary, pull developers away from their most valuable work: creating innovative solutions to business problems. As concerning as the lost time itself is the fragmentation of focus that creates a cognitive burden that directly impacts delivery quality and speed. Legacy processes often compound the challenge, generating low-value work that prevents deep, creative thinking.

The cost of context switching is taxing. When developers constantly pivot between writing application logic, debugging pipelines, investigating security alerts, and troubleshooting production issues, each transition extracts a mental cost. This cost doesn't just slow feature delivery—it fundamentally undermines the conditions that enable developer excellence. Deep, uninterrupted focus time drives software quality and innovation. When developers constantly jump between coding and operational tasks, both technical excellence and creative problem-solving suffer, leading to accumulated technical debt.

This issue impacts more than productivity metrics—it directly affects morale, retention, and the ability to attract top talent. The best engineering organizations understand that a great developer experience—where engineers can spend more time solving problems and less time wrestling with inefficiencies—not only leads to better software but also fosters a culture where top talent thrives and sticks around. A successful platform will address these sources of dissatisfaction, and developers will flock to it. If most developers must be forced to use a platform, there's likely something wrong with the platform or its rollout.

From Toolchains to Platform as a Product

Platform engineers address developer experience directly by creating an environment where developers can be maximally productive. This means designing, building, and maintaining the underlying developer platforms that enable the smooth development, deployment, and operation of applications and services.

Developer platforms typically address a number of areas, as shown in Figure 10-1. This includes a portal, CI/CD pipelines, and IaC. Automated measures to ensure security, compliance, and cloud cost compliance are woven throughout.

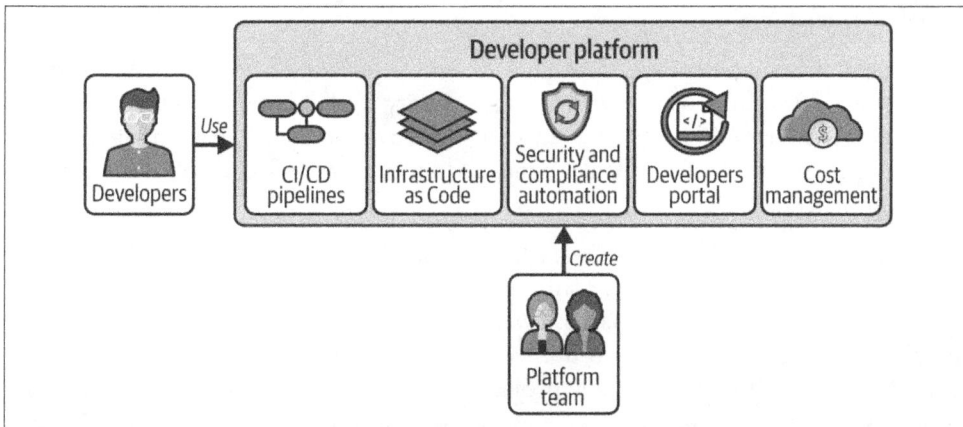

Figure 10-1. Developer platform capabilities

Developer platforms can be built in several ways: platform teams may assemble them from various tools, organizations can purchase prepackaged solutions from vendors like GitLab or Harness, or they can use orchestration tools like Humanitec to create a unified layer over existing toolsets. In practice, most implementations combine these approaches rather than following a single clean strategy. Teams usually pick a strategy and make some accommodations for things that are important to the organization but don't quite fit into the strategy. Being practical problem-solvers, engineers often blend strategies, adapting their chosen approach to accommodate crucial organizational needs, and ultimately they make it work.

Platforms present paved roads—proven patterns and practices that development teams can follow with confidence. Paved roads often take the form of application or infrastructure templates. Consider a standard web application template. Starting from scratch, developers might require several days to manually string together foundational capabilities and set up deployment—tedious and redundant work. A platform-provided template comes preconfigured with essential frameworks already in place. This includes standardized approaches for metrics collection, fault tolerance patterns, security configurations with sensible defaults, and structured logging with request tracing—all integrated within a cohesive framework. Templates can extend beyond application code to include infrastructure definitions and deployment pipeline configurations, forming a comprehensive application foundation.

In addition, platforms often offer templates that, at the application level, standardize approaches and encapsulate organizational best practices for cross-cutting concerns like authentication, logging, and error handling. The operational layer includes deployment pipelines that incorporate security scanning, load testing, and automated rollback procedures. The infrastructure layer leverages automation to provision resources with appropriate security groups, monitoring configurations, and disaster recovery procedures.

These capabilities are exposed through self-service portals or interfaces that abstract underlying complexity while maintaining security and compliance guardrails. For instance, a platform might provide an API for provisioning databases that automatically configures backup schedules, encryption, and access controls according to organizational standards.

The benefit is clear: rather than leaving teams to piece together tools, templates automate this tedious setup and configuration work while embedding best practices, security, and compliance standards. This makes developers more productive—with templated code in place, they can immediately focus on building features. Moreover, when they go to work on another project, whether because they've changed teams or because they need to update a dependency, they will be more comfortable and productive due to the familiar environment. Meanwhile, this added consistency reduces risk as it is easier to manage risks across a handful of standard tools and templates than a constellation of unique snowflakes scattered across the organization.

It's important to note that the specific templates and automations provided by a platform team will vary significantly from organization to organization. There's no one-size-fits-all approach. A platform team's focus must be laser-sharp on addressing the unique needs and use cases of its internal development teams. What works for a large financial institution with stringent compliance requirements will likely look very different from the platform built for a fast-moving startup. The key is for the platform team to deeply understand its "customers"—the development teams—and tailor its offerings to their specific pain points and workflows. Later in this chapter, we dig into the product mindset that platform engineering requires to ensure that the team is a true, developer experience–focused service provider to development teams.

The Business Case for Platform Engineering

The business case for platform engineering rests on a simple premise: by streamlining software development and operations, we can realize developer and operations productivity gains that make our teams more efficient and reduce the costs associated with risk. Consider the cost of developer time. If most developers spend roughly 30% of their time on repetitive, non-value-added tasks, for an organization with just 250 developers, this translates to substantial recoverable costs. Across companies we surveyed, developers earned an average of $107,599 annually, amounting to over $32,000 per developer in lost productivity annually. For organizations with 250 developers, this represents an $8 million hidden cost in lost development time.

Platform engineering provides developer platforms that automate many of these repetitive tasks, recovering lost time. Platform standardization and centralized platform development eliminate efforts duplicated across teams. This enables operations teams to support a larger application portfolio with existing headcount while maintaining consistent security and compliance standards.

The return on investment (ROI) of platform engineering extends beyond developer productivity. It addresses the business risks that keep teams up at night. Developer platform *paved roads* reduce the risk and potential cost of security breaches by eliminating security gaps that arise from inconsistent implementations across teams. With standardized deployment processes and monitoring practices, platform teams can reduce both the frequency and the impact of service outages. By embedding proven patterns for high availability and disaster recovery into platform components, organizations maintain business continuity even during incidents. Meanwhile, built-in compliance controls and automated audit trails help organizations avoid costly regulatory violations.

Platform engineering can also act as a powerful accelerator for broader organizational initiatives, such as cloud migrations or application modernization. By providing a standardized and automated foundation, platform engineering creates repeatable pathways that accelerate timelines while reducing risk.

Supporting a Collaborative DevOps Culture

Platform engineering supports collaboration between development, operations, and security teams, a theme we've returned to throughout previous chapters. A unified, self-service platform acts as a collaborative bridge. Instead of siloed responsibilities and potential friction points, platforms bring a more integrated ecosystem where operations and security requirements are addressed directly and automatically in platform paved roads. These paved roads give developers preapproved, secure patterns and automated workflows that inherently incorporate security best practices.

This is particularly powerful in regulated environments: instead of implementing new regulations for each application team, with the high probability that it won't be done consistently, the platform team can implement those rules once, at the platform level, ensuring compliance for everyone. Developers can focus on creating business value while automatically adhering to operational and security standards through platform guardrails. The net result is a more streamlined, secure software delivery pipeline.

Creating and Operating Platform Teams

Now that we understand the value of platform engineering (the "why"), we turn to implementation (the "how"). In this section, we'll examine how to establish and operate effective platform engineering teams. We'll look at the key characteristics of successful teams, discuss engagement models that keep platform teams closely aligned with development needs, and review operating models that support a scalable, high-performance platform engineering function.

Critical Characteristics of a Platform Team

The most successful platform engineering teams bring more than deep technical expertise—they bring product insight and customer empathy. Starting with platform leadership: leaders need the technical depth to understand the challenges developers face across the organization, while also possessing the strategic vision to align the platform with business goals. They must maintain credibility with both engineers and business stakeholders, bridging the gap between the technical and the strategic. Ideal leaders have a strong background in these three domains—development, operations, and security. This focus will help guide the team and organization in the right direction.

The platform team itself should be a microcosm of your development organization, encompassing expertise in development, security, and operations. This cross-functional knowledge allows the team to create integrated solutions that address the full spectrum of developer needs. The team should include engineers with experience in key bottleneck areas like security and compliance, in addition to engineers versed in development, enterprise architecture, and existing tools. As AI becomes a fundamental part of software delivery, platform teams benefit from including at least one member with expertise in AI/ML operations. This role bridges the gap between data science and software delivery, helping the team effectively integrate and manage AI-powered tools within the platform. They ensure AI components remain reliable, explainable, and aligned with organizational governance requirements.

Remember, the platform is a product, and developers are its customers. To ensure the platform evolves based on developer needs rather than platform team preferences alone, the team needs strong product management capabilities. This includes skills in user research, road map development, and adoption measurement. By understanding developer needs and measuring platform effectiveness, the team can ensure the platform remains a valuable asset for the entire organization.

Engagement Models That Work

One of the first considerations when starting a platform practice is determining how the team will engage with the larger organization. A successful platform team requires an engagement model that provides a deep understanding of developer needs and promotes effective collaboration across the organization. Platform teams must also engage with their customers—the development teams—in a thoughtful and structured manner.

An "immersion program" is an example of an engagement model that works well in some organizations. With this model, platform engineers temporarily embed themselves within individual development teams. The hands-on approach gives the teams insights into the daily challenges faced by developers; it fosters empathy and creates a deeper understanding of their needs. By working side-by-side with developers, platform engineers can identify pain points, bottlenecks, and opportunities for improvement. This ensures that the platform evolves in tandem with the unique needs of specific teams while still maintaining a central governance structure. This model can work particularly well when you are just getting started with platform engineering, as it helps form a deep understanding of team challenges and constraints.

Another option is to establish a Center of Excellence. This type of platform team operates as a distinct, cross-functional group serving all development teams. They provide feedback on platform features, advocate for adoption, and assist with the integration of platform capabilities into development workflows. Collaboration across the organization ensures that the platform remains aligned with the evolving needs of the development community. This model works well for larger organizations with diverse projects, as it provides clear ownership and centralized best practices while reducing the duplication of effort.

Alternatively, hybrid models, where platform engineers serve both as centralized experts and as embedded resources, offer the best of both worlds—consistency in tooling and processes coupled with intimate knowledge of specific product challenges.

Choosing the right model depends on your organization's size, complexity, and strategic priorities. The stage of your platform maturity can also be a factor. As the platform matures and the user base grows, the engagement model needs to scale. While high-touch support might be feasible for early adopters, a more scalable approach is necessary for widespread adoption. Self-service onboarding, enabled by comprehensive documentation and intuitive tools, allows teams to integrate with the platform seamlessly and autonomously.

Lastly, while each of these models provides a structural foundation for platform success, they must be reinforced by robust mechanisms to measure and validate platform effectiveness. Later in this chapter we'll look at ensuring that systematic feedback loops are in place to measure developer satisfaction and platform adoption.

Effective Operating Models

While the engagement model guides how the platform team interacts with development teams, the operating model defines the platform team's internal processes and principles. The operating model is crucial for serving development teams while maintaining high operational standards. It dictates how the team functions, allocates resources, and interacts with the broader organization. An effective model strikes a balance between empowerment and control.

A strong operating model prioritizes self-service capabilities that empower development teams to move quickly and independently. The platform team maintains appropriate guardrails through automation and template offerings that encapsulate best practices for the organization.

Clear, up-to-date, and readily accessible documentation is another feature of an effective operating model. Documentation should empower developers to understand and adopt platform capabilities without requiring hand-holding from the platform team.

Finally, your operating model should be structured to handle both tactical and strategic needs—implementing SLAs for critical issues while protecting dedicated time for platform improvements and addressing developer feedback. Techniques like support rotations and engineering sprints can help teams manage this balance.

Defining Your Platform Strategy

A coherent platform strategy is squarely focused on your developer needs. It takes into account the constraints of your organization and the objectives most important to your business. In this section we'll discuss how your strategy should clearly articulate a set of principles that will guide decision making. We'll explore how a deep understanding of your platform customers should drive the initial scope. Lastly, we'll discuss the challenges you may encounter in balancing standardization through the platform with flexibility in allowing teams to diverge when needed.

Setting Platform Principles

Platform strategy starts with clear principles that articulate how your platform team will approach solutions. When the team is getting pulled in many different directions and is asked to address a growing set of concerns, clear principles act as a compass. They guide decision making and provide a framework for evaluating trade-offs, resolving conflicts, and maintaining focus amid the complexities of platform development. Once you have defined your principles, it's important to share them throughout your organization to get the alignment that will help the team be successful.

The following principles are ones that should underpin any platform strategy:

Developer experience and effectiveness is the primary driver of platform design.
Every capability should aim to reduce cognitive load and streamline development workflows, rather than adding complexity.

Security and compliance requirements are embedded seamlessly into the platform.
This makes it easier for developers to "do things right" than to bypass controls. The approach fosters a secure development environment without hindering productivity.

Platform evolution is driven by measurable developer needs and demonstrable business outcomes.
Platform evolution is not driven only by the technical preferences of the platform team or the strong opinions of any given developer team. The platform team will solicit feedback from developers, track platform usage, and measure the impact on key metrics like deployment frequency and lead time.

A key strategic decision is whether adoption should be mandatory or optional. Mandatory platforms can drive consistency and standardization, but risk reducing the incentive to deliver a great developer experience. Optional adoption, on the other hand, forces the platform team to earn trust and prove value, leading to more user-focused, innovative solutions. While this approach can create fragmentation, it fosters excellence in practice, not just in theory. Some organizations begin with optional adoption and introduce mandates later to consolidate gains and bring late adopters on board.

Platform Antiprinciples and Resolving Conflicts

Just as important as what your platform strategy should embrace is what it should avoid. Common antiprinciples that undermine platform success include:

Perfectionism over progress
Delaying platform releases until they're "perfect" often means developers create their own solutions in the meantime, making eventual adoption harder.

Technology-driven development
> Building platform capabilities because they're technically interesting or cool rather than because they solve real developer problems.

Mandatory adoption without demonstrating value
> Forcing teams to use the platform before proving its value creates resistance and potentially damages the platform's reputation long term.

When principles come into tension with each other, as they inevitably will, having a clear prioritization framework helps. For example, when security requirements conflict with developer experience, most organizations need a structured approach to resolve this tension. Successful platform teams typically prioritize:

1. Security and compliance requirements that carry regulatory risk
2. Developer experience for high-frequency activities
3. Standardization for operational consistency
4. Innovation and flexibility

This hierarchy helps teams make consistent decisions when principles compete. When facing such conflicts, platform teams should document the tension, the decision-making process, and the eventual resolution to create precedent for future decisions.

Allowing a model like this to support a choice that results in poor developer experience in the name of security is dangerous. You have planted a seed for circumventing or manipulating the platform. Treating such a decision as a necessary stopgap, and then working to develop a more efficient and pleasant way of satisfying the governance control, is a key to long-term success.

Understanding Your Platform Audience

Going back to our first principle: developer experience and effectiveness is the primary driver of platform design. A successful platform strategy starts with a deep understanding of your development teams' needs and the broader organizational context. The immersion engagement model can help here. With this model platform engineers embed in individual application teams for a time period. By sitting next to application developers and learning about their work through close observation and asking questions, platform team members are better able to identify common friction points, bottlenecks, and opportunities for improvement. Consider both immediate pain points hindering developer productivity and long-term strategic objectives.

Selecting Platform Scope

Once you've started to develop a clear picture of your platform audience, the next step is to define the initial scope of your platform capabilities. The most effective approach is to start small by focusing on foundational elements that immediately unlock developer productivity. Streamlined infrastructure provisioning, automated delivery pipelines, and integrated security automation are good examples. As your platform matures and the organization's needs evolve, you can incrementally expand into more advanced areas, like creating a comprehensive developer portal or introducing self-service analytics tools. The key is to resist the temptation to solve every problem at once—successful platforms grow steadily, guided by demonstrated value and continuous feedback from the teams they serve.

A Practical Road Map Example

Let's walk through a practical example of using an understanding of our audience to select initial scope. A useful approach is to zero in on the teams and use cases that are already driving rapid innovation. For example, teams that are adopting new technologies or making the leap to cloud platforms often face acute challenges that even a simple platform can help quickly resolve.

In our example, we decide to focus our efforts to support an applications team transitioning to microservices on AWS and Kubernetes. This team is struggling with standardized infrastructure and deployment patterns. By addressing this specific need, we can demonstrate the platform's value and gain traction within our organization. In identifying our earlier adopter team, we are careful to select a team that is enthusiastic about actively collaborating in refining the platform offering and willing to provide frequent feedback.

In this case, we start by creating a paved road that streamlines common tasks. We automate the creation of a new microservice from repository creation through CI/CD pipeline configuration and infrastructure provisioning. Out of the gate, this doesn't need to encompass every tool in the pipeline. We focus on including only the core build, deploy, and governance layers, and we embed organizational standards directly into our template. In accordance with our second principle, security requirements, compliance controls, and operational best practices are baked in. We partner closely with compliance and security teams to ensure our automated patterns meet their requirements. The goal is that by using our platform, application teams default to doing the right thing.

Another suggestion for an easy win is to consider offering application teams audit help as a service as part of your platform. Build in functionality that automates answering certain audit questions on their behalf. Because you're building the system with internal audit in mind, this will be easy to provide and will help drive adoption and delight your users.

Balancing Standardization and Flexibility

In establishing a platform engineering practice, you may find challenges in standardizing software delivery with your platform paths and giving the teams the flexibility they need (or just want). Consistent software delivery, through standardized platform paths, is what ensures the platform's reliability, operational efficiency, and ultimately its business value. However, your platform should allow some team autonomy; teams should be able to innovate to come up with the most appropriate and efficient solutions for their specific needs. An overly opinionated template with very rigid paths will only deter adoption of your platform.

One way to approach this challenge is to consider the components of your template in these three categories:

Mandatory components
> This set of components addresses functions like logging configuration, monitoring setup, and security controls. These are mission-critical concerns (security, observability, compliance) and are strictly standardized. Their inclusion is enforced.

Configurable components
> These components include resource scaling configuration, cache settings, and database connections. Teams should be able to configure as needed without impacting overall objectives of standardization.

Extension points
> Finally, extension points should be used to allow teams to customize aspects such as health checks, configure specialized middleware, and define team-specific metrics. Well-documented APIs provide these extension points, defining clear interfaces between standardized and flexible components.

With this modular approach, teams can use paved path templates while having the flexibility to adapt them to their needs. A team building a high-throughput service might customize the scaling configuration and add specialized performance metrics, while a team building a security-sensitive service might add extra authentication middleware and audit logging.

The role of governance in this balance is crucial. Effective platforms use PaC and automated validation to create guardrails that prevent serious issues while allowing deviation within safe boundaries. For instance, instead of mandating every technology choice, you might implement automated checks that verify that key requirements are met, regardless of the specific implementation. This approach allows teams to innovate while ensuring essential standards are maintained.

Platform Measurement and Evolution

With a platform strategy in place, the next step is to measure its effectiveness and drive its adoption. This section explores how to define and track metrics to demonstrate platform value and then examines strategies for encouraging developer engagement and platform utilization.

Measuring Platform Success

You can't improve what you don't measure. Think of your platform as a product with both technical and business KPIs. Indicators should help you assess value to both developers and the business. Key metric categories include:

Developer productivity
> How much faster can teams ship features using the platform? Track metrics like deployment frequency, lead time for changes, and MTTR. Use metrics to get a better understanding of time spent writing code versus managing infrastructure.

Platform adoption
> Are teams actually using the platform? Metrics should measure both breadth (the number of active users, projects leveraging the platform, and the percentage of new projects onboarded) and depth (how extensively teams leverage available features). Usage patterns here can help identify both successful offerings and potential friction points.

Operational efficiency
> How much has the platform reduced costs or improved operational performance? Look at infrastructure costs, incident rates, and support ticket volume.

Business impact
> Ultimately, does the platform contribute to business goals? Metrics should connect platform investments to organizational outcomes such as faster time-to-market, increased customer satisfaction, or improved product quality.

We track platform performance and value creation to validate continuous improvement and guide platform initiatives. Next, we'll explore strategies to encourage initial platform adoption and facilitate platform evolution to unlock further value.

Driving Platform Adoption

Armed with a clear vision for our platform informed by understanding of our audience's most acute pain points, our next challenge lies in driving adoption of our platform. A well-executed adoption strategy combines careful capability selection, seamless access, and proactive engagement.

A minimum viable platform (MVP) approach is one that will help drive early adoption. Instead of trying to build everything at once, focus platform work on delivering a small set of high-value, low-effort capabilities that address the most pressing pain points for development teams. These initial wins build credibility and demonstrate our platform's potential, making it easier to secure buy-in and resources for future expansion. Based on the understanding we've gained about our audience, consider the tasks that consume the most developer time or cause the most friction. By tackling these challenges first, we can quickly show tangible benefits and generate excitement around the platform.

Finally, if you are a platform team you must actively market your capabilities. Building a great platform is only half the battle; you also need to convince developers to use it. Consider developer education programs, technical showcases, and clear communication of the platform benefits and road map. Host workshops and training sessions to teach developers how to use the platform effectively. Showcase successful use cases and highlight the positive impact the platform has had on other teams. Maintain a clear road map and communicate upcoming features and improvements to build excitement and encourage adoption. By actively engaging with the developer community, platform teams can foster a culture of adoption and ensure the platform becomes an integral part of the development workflow.

Leveraging Internal Developer Portals for Platform Success

Internal developer portals (IDPs) serve as the interface between development teams and your platform capabilities. Portals make the platform easy to discover and use by bringing everything together in one place. The most effective portals include service discovery, contextual documentation, and self-service capabilities, making them the natural starting point for any developer interaction with the platform.

Core portal components

A well-designed IDP typically includes:

Software catalog
    A centralized registry of all services, APIs, and components with ownership information and dependency mapping

Self-service workflows
    Automated processes for common tasks like creating new services or provisioning environments using "golden path" templates

Documentation hub
    Contextual, searchable technical resources that appear when needed

Scorecards
> Metrics showing service maturity, compliance status, and adoption of best practices

AI-enhanced developer experience

Modern IDPs increasingly leverage the following AI capabilities to reduce cognitive load and accelerate platform adoption:

Natural language interfaces
> Allow developers to find resources and execute workflows using conversational queries.

Intelligent recommendations
> Suggest relevant documentation, services, and configuration options based on the developer's context and history.

Automated troubleshooting
> Analyze error patterns and suggest potential solutions when developers encounter issues.

Predictive assistance
> Anticipate developer needs based on their current activities and proactively offer relevant resources.

These AI capabilities transform the portal from a passive resource to an active assistant that guides developers through complex operations without requiring them to become experts.

Building an effective portal

For sustainable success, treat your IDP as a product with dedicated resources for its ongoing development. Measure its effectiveness through metrics like developer adoption rates, time saved through self-service workflows, and new developer time-to-productivity.

IDPs have recently become available off the shelf. Backstage, developed initially at Spotify, was open sourced and donated to the Cloud Native Computing Foundation in 2020. Commercial offerings to simplify Backstage adoption and management have emerged from vendors including Roadie, Spotify, and Harness. Non-Backstage commercial IDPs are also available, such as Atlassian's Compass.

A well-designed IDP reduces cognitive load, accelerates onboarding, and makes platform adoption the path of least resistance, transforming how developers experience your entire platform offering.

Sustainable Platform Evolution

With initial adoption underway, the next step is ensuring the platform's sustainable evolution. This hinges on balancing developer empowerment with platform integrity, achieved through PaC and automation, continuous feedback loops, and continual investment in reliability and scalability. Leveraging PaC that enables "trust but verify" automation is one way to achieve this balance. By encoding organizational standards into programmable policies (using tools like OPA or custom enforcement engines), your platform team can delegate control while maintaining compliance.

Policy and Policy as Code can give some control to development teams to reduce bottlenecks and foster agility without sacrificing standardization. For example, policies can define acceptable resource usage limits, enforce security best practices, or ensure compliance with organizational standards. Developers can operate within predefined boundaries, knowing that their actions won't compromise the stability or security of the platform. Crucially, policies can also be used to signal upcoming changes, such as deprecating older systems or templates. By issuing warnings well in advance, developers have time to migrate to newer, supported options, ensuring a smooth transition and minimizing disruption when the older systems are eventually retired.

AI technology is evolving rapidly, creating both opportunities and challenges for platform teams. It's crucial to establish a systematic approach to evaluating emerging AI tools before incorporating them into your platform. Create a sandbox environment where promising technologies can be tested against real-world scenarios using your organization's data. Develop clear criteria for graduating AI capabilities from experimental to production-ready, including considerations around reliability, explainability, and governance. This approach allows your platform to benefit from AI advancements while managing the risks of rapidly evolving technology.

Platform evolution must be guided by empirical evidence rather than assumptions. Your team must make a regular practice of reviewing your "platform intelligence triangle"—the combination of platform usage metrics, support requests, and developer feedback. Use these to guide road map development and identify developer needs and pain points. Are certain features underutilized? Are there common support requests that indicate areas for improvement? For instance, if you notice increasing support tickets around a particular service coupled with declining usage patterns, it might indicate a reliability issue that requires immediate attention. Regular platform health checks should examine both technical metrics (error rates, response times) and adoption metrics (feature usage, team onboarding success).

Finally, consistent investment in platform reliability and scalability is nonnegotiable—a single significant outage can erase months of trust-building. As platform adoption grows—and platform load increases—investment in reliability engineering becomes more critical. Developers need to trust that the platform will be available when they need it and that it will perform consistently. This includes implementing robust observability, establishing clear incident management processes, and maintaining transparent communication channels with development teams.

A Practical Example: Platform Engineering in Action

As an example, consider a financial services organization with 1,400 developers spread across 80 product teams facing significant delivery challenges. An audit revealed inconsistent security practices, and the CTO was concerned about both velocity and compliance risks. Meanwhile, internal metrics showed developers spending nearly 45% of their time on noncoding activities—managing pipelines, configuring environments, and addressing security and compliance requirements.

To address these challenges, the organization formed a dedicated platform team consisting of six people: a platform engineering lead, a senior developer with CI/CD expertise, a security engineer, an operations engineer, a platform engineer with Kubernetes expertise, and a technical product manager who would also handle documentation.

Discovery and strategy development

The team began with an intensive discovery phase to understand both developer pain points and compliance requirements. They implemented a structured immersion program, embedding team members with representative product teams to observe workflows and document challenges. This research revealed common pain points:

- Duplicated effort in maintaining separate CI/CD pipelines across teams
- Inconsistent security scanning implementation
- Manual environment provisioning creating delays and inconsistencies
- Poorly understood compliance requirements implemented differently across teams

Simultaneously, the team engaged with governance stakeholders through working sessions with the CISO's team, enterprise architecture, compliance, and legal to understand security controls, technical standards, audit requirements, and data handling requirements.

Based on this research, the team developed a platform strategy with clear principles:

- Developer experience drives platform design—reducing cognitive load.
- Security and compliance are built in, not bolted on.
- Everything is measurable—focusing only on what delivers value.
- The platform is optional but compelling—solving real problems.

The team deliberately focused their initial scope on a single high-impact capability: secure CI/CD pipelines with embedded security controls.

Building the minimum viable platform

The team delivered their MVP within eight weeks: a template-driven pipeline system with embedded security scanning. Key components included:

- Pipeline templates with best practices for different application types
- Preconfigured security scanning integrated directly into the pipeline
- Automated evidence collection for compliance requirements
- Self-service configuration through a simple YAML file

The team embedded required security controls directly into the pipeline templates, with static analysis, dependency scanning, container scanning, and compliance checks running automatically. Results fed into a centralized dashboard, while automated evidence collection simplified audit preparation.

With key checks automated, including required levels of code coverage, the change management process was streamlined dramatically for application teams on the platform. They were excited to be granted an exemption from going to the CAB.

Working closely with two pilot teams, the platform team refined their offering based on weekly feedback. Documentation was developed alongside the code, with both technical reference material and practical guides.

Within three months, the MVP showed impressive results with pilot teams:

- Deployment time reduced from five days to six hours.
- Security scanning coverage increased from 40% to 100%.
- Audit preparation time reduced from days to hours.
- Critical vulnerabilities discovered and remediated through automated scanning.

By the six-month mark, 15 teams (about 250 engineers) were using the secure pipeline templates, and security incidents from these teams had dropped by 40%, compared with nonadopting teams.

Expanding platform capabilities

Based on comprehensive telemetry and user feedback, the platform team identified environment provisioning as their next target. They also recognized that with growing adoption, they needed a more scalable approach to onboarding and support.

Their next phase focused on two key capabilities:

- An IDP that served as a single interface for all platform capabilities, including:
  — A service catalog with automated discovery
  — Self-service onboarding for secure pipelines
  — Integrated documentation and guides
  — Real-time visibility into pipeline status and security findings
- IaC templates for common application patterns that encoded best practices for:
  — Secure network configuration
  — Properly configured access controls
  — Compliance-aligned logging and monitoring
  — Resource limits and cost controls

These templates integrated with the IDP, allowing developers to provision compliant environments with minimal effort.

The expanded platform dramatically increased adoption. Within six months:

- 45 teams (representing around 600 developers) were using the secure pipelines.
- 30 teams had adopted the IaC templates for environment provisioning.
- The platform handled over 2,000 deployments per month.
- Support requests per user had dropped by 70% due to self-service capabilities.

The platform team continued to operate with just six people despite serving hundreds of developers, leveraging self-service capabilities and automation to scale their impact.

Enterprise-wide adoption and business impact

To drive broader adoption, the platform team developed a multifaceted approach:

- Internal events showcasing capabilities and success stories
- A "Platform Champions" program identifying advocates in each department
- Executive dashboards showing adoption metrics and business impact
- Training programs with both self-paced and instructor-led options

The CTO established incentives for adoption, with platform users receiving priority for cloud resources and streamlined compliance reviews.

As platform adoption grew, governance approaches evolved. Instead of manual reviews and documentation, security and compliance requirements were encoded directly into the platform through:

- PaC frameworks that automatically enforced standards
- Built-in evidence collection that satisfied audit requirements
- Self-service exception processes for legitimate edge cases
- Automated compliance reporting from platform telemetry

By the 18-month mark, the platform had achieved significant results:

- 85% of development teams (representing around 1,200 developers) using the platform.
- Developer productivity increased by 35%.
- Deployment frequency increased 6× across the organization.
- Mean time to recover from failures decreased by 70%.
- Security incidents reduced by 65% for platform users.
- Audit preparation time reduced by 90%.
- Time-to-market for new features reduced by 40%.

These improvements translated to tangible business outcomes: faster feature releases, quicker responses to market changes, reduced downtime, and lower security and compliance risks.

Ongoing improvements

Three years into the journey, the platform team continually evolved its offerings. Their road map included AI-assisted development capabilities, advanced observability tools, expanded security automation, and developer experience improvements based on ongoing research.

The key lessons from this platform engineering journey included:

Product mindset is essential
    Treating developers as customers drives better decisions.

Starting small builds credibility
    Deliver one capability well before expanding.

Self-service is key to scale
    Adopt an agile approach, delivering iteratively.

Metrics drive investment
    Measure both technical outcomes and business impact.

Governance integration creates win-wins
    The right tooling can turn compliance from a constraint into an accelerator.

This example demonstrates how a small, focused platform team can drive significant organizational transformation by systematically addressing developer needs while streamlining governance requirements. By starting with high-impact capabilities, measuring outcomes, and treating the platform as a product, the team achieved remarkable scale, serving 1,400 developers with just six platform engineers.

Conclusion

As we wrap up our exploration of modern software delivery, one thing is clear: AI isn't just another tool in our DevOps toolkit; it's fundamentally changing how we build and deliver software.

Throughout this book, we've seen how AI is impacting every stage of the software lifecycle. From detecting code patterns in repositories to optimizing test selection, from identifying security vulnerabilities to automating cloud cost optimization, AI capabilities are rapidly becoming integral to modern delivery practices.

Platform engineering ties these elements together, creating a foundation where AI-powered capabilities work in concert to accelerate delivery while maintaining governance. By building developer platforms that abstract complexity and embed best practices, teams can focus more on creating business value and less on the undifferentiated heavy lifting that has traditionally consumed so much developer time.

At the time of writing, AI for developer coding assistants is more mature than AI for many parts of software delivery. This promises to put new strains on DevOps teams as innovation becomes increasingly constrained not on an organization's ability to generate code, but on its ability to validate and deliver those applications. Delivery excellence, increasingly dependent on AI, will be a key factor in who will take full advantage of advances in coding techniques and who will be frustrated.

Looking Forward

The shift to AI-native delivery practices is still in its early stages, but the direction is unmistakable. Organizations that effectively integrate AI into their delivery pipelines will gain significant advantages:

- Accelerated delivery cycles as AI eliminates bottlenecks and automates routine tasks
- Improved quality and security through AI-powered testing and vulnerability detection
- Reduced operational costs via intelligent resource optimization and automated remediation
- Enhanced developer experience as cognitive load shifts from operational concerns to creative problem-solving

In practice, this means deployment decisions will increasingly be made based on sophisticated AI analysis rather than human judgment alone. Test strategies will adapt dynamically to code changes instead of following rigid patterns. Infrastructure will self-optimize based on application needs rather than requiring manual tuning.

Getting Started

If you're looking to implement these practices in your organization, we recommend a pragmatic approach:

- Identify your most painful bottlenecks first. Where are your teams spending the most time on low-value activities? These are your prime targets for AI-powered automation.
- Start small and measure relentlessly. Implement focused improvements, validate their impact, and use that success to drive further adoption.
- Build for your developers, not for the tools. Adopt a product mindset for your delivery platform, ensuring it actually solves real problems for your teams.
- Embed governance, don't bolt it on. Use your platform to make compliance and security seamless parts of the development process, not afterthoughts.

The organizations that thrive in this new era won't necessarily be those with the largest engineering teams or the biggest budgets. Rather, they'll be the ones that most effectively harness AI to deliver better software, faster, while maintaining the governance guardrails necessary for enterprise operation.

This won't happen overnight. Like any significant transformation, it requires committed leadership, continuous learning, and a willingness to challenge established processes. But the rewards—measured in development velocity, product quality, and ultimately business outcomes—make this journey worth undertaking.

The future of software delivery is intelligent, automated, and built for the needs of the human developers who remain at its core. We hope this book has provided you with both the technical understanding and the practical strategies to begin building that future in your organization today.

Index

autonomous deployment decisions, 115
building and testing software (history of CI), 32-34
CD deployment and test process, 53-64
CD promotion between environments, 64-67
chaos engineering integration, 106-110
CI process, 34-41
CI tools, 41-50
in Gitflow, 18
IaCM, 66
observability/deployment integration, 126
security risk identification, 77-79
and trunk-based development, 131
circuit breakers, 97
Cloud Carbon Footprint, 159
cloud computing, development of, 146
cloud cost management, 145-160
  AI-driven optimization strategies, 149-155
  AI's future in, 160
  business objectives alignment in, 155
  challenges for, 149
  evolution of, 146-149
  governance and compliance automation, 155-158
  sustainability goals, 158-159
cloud resource allocation, 150-151
cloud service connection strings, 23
cloud-hosted solution, CI/CD pipelines, 45
cloud-native architectures, 6
CloudFormation, 56
clusters, container, 154
CMake build tool, 36
Codacy, 25
code repositories, 14
  (see also GitOps)
  centralized versus distributed VCS, 15-17
  and monorepos, 50
  repository as single source of truth, 20
  SCM, 23-29
  secret detection, 23
code reviews, 25
code smells, static analysis, 38
code trigger step, CI process, 35, 58
Codecov supply chain hack, 72
CollabNet, 14
collaboration and code review, IaC for, 55
collaborative DevOps culture, 167
commitment-based pricing, 151-154
Committed Use Contracts, 152

common vulnerabilities and exposures (CVEs), 79
communication and collaboration, DevOps, 2
compute resources (virtual machines and containers), 150
Concurrent Versions System (CVS), 14
configuration drift, 98, 106
configuration-as-code, 24
consumerization of enterprise technology, 7
container image, 75, 83
containers and containerization, 7
  cloud cost management in, 154-155
  orchestration software support for rolling updates, 120
  tools to support, 44
context switching cost for development teams, 164
continuous behavioral monitoring, supply chain security, 84
continuous delivery versus continuous deployment, 59
continuous integration/continuous deployment and delivery (see CI/CD pipeline)
continuous resilience, CI/CD pipeline, 106-109
control plane overload simulation, 102
core repository, pipeline role of, 21
cost allocation
  implementing for sustainability, 159
  shared platforms and services, 158
  tagging for accurate, 157
cost management (see cloud cost management)
CRA (Cyber Resilience Act), 73
credential hygiene, insufficient, 78
cross-domain identity management (SCIM), 142
CruiseControl, 33
cryptography practices, 91
Cunningham, Ward, 32
Cursor, 21
CVEs (common vulnerabilities and exposures), 79
CVS (Concurrent Version System), 14
Cyber Resilience Act (CRA), 73
cyberthreat landscape for applications, 70-74, 91
CycloneDX, 87

FinOps, 145
    and containerization, 154
    phases of, 147-149
    principles of, 146-147
    right-sizing cloud resources, 150-151
Forsgren, Nicole, 5, 114
fully-managed solutions, CI/CD, 44-46
functional testing, 60, 62

G

General Data Protection Regulation (GDPR),
    74
generative AI (GenAI), ix
    caching techniques for CI/CD pipeline, 47
    in chaos engineering, 96
    providing insights in build and test phases,
    49
Git, 15-17, 25
Gitflow, 17-19
GitHub, 17, 25
GitHub Copilot, 21
GitLab, 26
GitOps
    automating Git changes, 19, 66
    deployment process with Git workflows,
    56-57
    repositories (see code repositories)
    SCM, 19
governance
    automated audit trails and enforcement, 142
    chaos engineering, 109
    cloud cost management, 155-158
    need for, 9
    platform approach, 26, 174, 179
    production deployment, 112-119
    in sustainable platform evolution, 178
Gradle build tool, 37
Groovy scripts, 42
Groovy-based DSL, 37
Grunt task runner, 37
guardrail metrics for progressive delivery,
    137-138
Gulp task runner, 37

H

hallucination squatting, by cyber attackers, 72,
    85
Harness, 5, 126, 177
    AI Code Agent, 21

CCM, 151
Chaos Engineering, 99, 110
CI, 50
Cloud Cost Management, 159
Code Repository, 25
FinOps Agent, 153
Platform, 28
Software Engineering Insights, 25
Test Intelligence (TI), 48
Harness.io, 26
hollowing-out-the-middle approach to testing,
    63-64
Humble, Jez, 5, 114
hybrid cost management, 149
hypervisors, 45

I

IaC (Infrastructure as Code), 55-56, 76, 181
IaCM (Infrastructure as Code Management)
    tools, 66, 122
IBM Rational ClearCase, 14
identity and access management, security issue,
    77
identity management infrastructure, feature
    flags, 142
IDPs (internal developer portals), 176-177, 181
IEEE 829 Standard for Software and System
    Test Documentation (1983), 32
immersion engagement, platform engineering,
    169, 172
inferences versus attestations, and artifact trust-
    worthiness, 83
Inform phase, FinOps, 147, 150
Information Technology Infrastructure Library
    (ITIL), 113-114
Infrastructure as Code (IaC), 55-56, 76, 181
Infrastructure as Code Management (IaCM)
    tools, 66, 122
infrastructure failure, chaos engineering experi-
    ments in, 100
input validation cyberthreat, 91
instances, container, 154
insufficient flow control mechanisms, CI/CD
    pipelines, 77
integration tests, 35, 39, 41
intent-based tests, 49, 62
internal developer portals (IDPs), 176-177, 181
iOS, XCTest for, 40
ISO/IEC 27036-2:2023, 73

ITIL (Information Technology Infrastructure Library), 113-114

J
Java
    automated testing, 39
    build tools for, 37
Java-based architecture, Jenkins's efficiency concerns, 43
JavaScript
    Jest and Mocha for testing, 39
    task runners for, 37
Jeffries, Ron, 32
Jenkins, 33, 42-46
Jest and Mocha, JavaScript testing, 39
JUnit 5 and TestNG frameworks, Java, 39
JUnit framework, 33

K
Kawaguchi, Kohsuke, 33
Kibana, 49
Kim, Gene, 5, 114
Knight Capital trading incident, 111, 129
known vulnerabilities, OSS, 79
Kubernetes, 5, 44
    autoscaling functionality, 155
    chaos engineering testing tools, 101
    container orchestrating with GitOps tools, 57
    rolling updates support, 120

L
Lambda, 5
latency experiment, chaos engineering, 97
leadership, characteristics of platform, 168
lean manufacturing, and Agile, 3
license risk, 80
linters, CI static analysis, 38
LitmusChaos, 99
load balancers, for rolling updates, 120
load testing, and shift-right approach, 63
localization testing, 61
Log4j, 71
logs and logging
    insufficient visibility, 79
    Jenkins challenges in CI pipelines, 43
    as observability pillar, 125
Logstash, 49
long short-term memory (LSTM), 149

long-lived feature branches, 131

M
machine learning (ML), 5
    (see also AI)
main branch, Gitflow, 17
Make build tool, 36
marketing platform capabilities for developers, 176
Maven build tool, 37
MCP (Model Context Protocol), 10, 25, 47
metrics
    CFR, 106
    in feature experimentation, 135
    guardrails for progressive delivery, 137-138
    and observability, 49, 125
    platform engineering success, 175
    recovery time, 106
microservices architectures, 6, 20-21, 124
Microsoft Azure Resource Manager, 56
minimum viable platform (MVP) approach, 176, 180
ML (machine learning), 5
    (see also AI)
mobile app development, CI/CD pipeline, 44-46
mobile testing tools, 40
Model Context Protocol (MCP), 10, 25, 47
monolithic software, deployment and rollback complexities, 124
monorepo architectures, 20, 48, 49
MSBuild build tool, 37
"multiarmed bandit" machine learning approach, 134
multicloud cost management, 149
MVP (minimum viable platform) approach, 176, 180

N
name confusion attacks, 80
National Telecommunications and Information Administration (NTIA) Multistakeholder Process, 87
natural language interfaces, cloud cost management with AI, 160
.NET frameworks, 37, 39
Netflix, 93, 95
network disruption, chaos engineering experiments in, 99

About the Authors

Nick Durkin is field CTO for Harness, with responsibility for the organization's worldwide field engineering team, postsales engineering team, and a portion of the platform. He previously held technical and executive roles at OverOps, DataTorrent, and Zelle (Early Warning), where he ran critical infrastructure for the United States government. He also served as lead architect on the Department of Homeland Security's Financial Institution—Verifying Identity Credential Service (FIVICS) initiative, where he developed several patents for antifraud technologies, which are currently in use not only by the federal government but also by some of the world's largest financial institutions.

Eric Minick is senior director of DevOps solutions at Harness, with a focus on enabling AI-native pipelines and developer experience. For over two decades, he has helped global enterprises, including IBM and UrbanCode, adopt DevOps practices at scale. He regularly contributes to the DevOps community through writing, speaking, and consulting.

Chinmay Gaikwad is director of product marketing at Harness, where he combines deep AI-native DevOps and AppSec expertise with strategic marketing leadership. He is a software engineer by training and is recognized for his expertise in application security, DevOps practices, and developer experience, with a proven track record in both technical and marketing roles across early-stage and late-stage startups as well as public companies.

Colophon

The animal on the cover of *AI-Native Software Delivery* is a pastel ringwrasse (*Hologymnosus doliatus*). A vibrant marine fish species commonly found in the tropical waters of the Indo-Pacific region, particularly around coral reefs from the Red Sea and East Africa to the Central Pacific, the pastel ringwrasse inhabits lagoons and reef slopes at depths ranging from 1 to 60 meters, favoring sandy or rubble substrates adjacent to coral formations. This wrasse is easily recognizable by its elongated, slender body adorned with iridescent pastel shades of blue, green, and pink, along with distinctive horizontal stripes and—as the name suggests—ring-like patterns. Males typically display more vibrant coloration and larger size.

The pastel ringwrasse is a carnivorous species that primarily feeds on small crustaceans, mollusks, and other invertebrates, which it forages from the seabed using its pointed snout. Known for being active during the day, it is a solitary or loosely schooling fish that exhibits secretive behavior when threatened, darting quickly into crevices. Like many wrasses, the pastel ringwrasse starts life as female and can change to male as part of a complex social structure. The species has a relatively long lifespan for a reef fish, living up to 10 years in the wild. Wrasses do not exhibit parental care; instead, spawning occurs through broadcast fertilization, with eggs and larvae left to drift in the plankton until they settle. Currently, the pastel ringwrasse is not listed as endangered and is categorized as Least Concern by the International Union for Conservation of Nature (IUCN), although it can be affected by habitat degradation and collection for the aquarium trade.

Many of the animals on O'Reilly covers are endangered; all of them are important to the world.

The cover illustration is by José Marzan Jr., based on a black-and-white engraving from *English Cyclopedia*. The series design is by Edie Freedman, Ellie Volckhausen, and Karen Montgomery. The cover fonts are Gilroy Semibold and Guardian Sans. The text font is Adobe Minion Pro; the heading font is Adobe Myriad Condensed; and the code font is Dalton Maag's Ubuntu Mono.

www.ingramcontent.com/pod-product-compliance
Lightning Source LLC
Chambersburg PA
CBHW061419210326
41598CB00035B/6273